CONTENTS

Marriage

Parenting

family

Marriage

Why Do We Marry?

$\mathcal{T}$HERE is nothing in the world so attractive as someone who will dream with us, merge their dreams with our own, clarify the path toward the actualization of the dream, and lock their arms into ours while walking the path.

Neil Clark Warren
The Triumphant Marriage

THE story of a love is not important—what is important is that one is capable of love. It is perhaps the only glimpse we are permitted of eternity.

Helen Hayes
in *Guideposts* magazine (1960)

ONE of the reasons people get married is suntan lotion; you're going to need help. There are parts of your back that you simply can't get to by yourself, and quite frankly, no one is going to do it for you who isn't married to you.

Paul Reiser
Couplehood

THE men that women marry,
And why they marry them, will always be
A marvel and mystery to the world.

Henry Wadsworth Longfellow

THE moment two young people have made the mutual confession that their supreme happiness is wrapped up in each other, they are within measurable distance of the great crisis of their lives.

Christine Terhune Herrick
The Modern Hostess

ONE of the goals of Christian marriage is to "reverse the curse" of the husband ruling over the wife and the wife seeking to overthrow his leadership.

David Stoop
Seeking God Together

UNMET needs and tension are traveling companions. Sometimes our needs can be satisfied through natural means—other times, God's supernatural touch is required. Open your heart to receive from Him, then get ready, for only God—not romance—can fill the holes in your soul.

Jean Lush
"Isn't It Romantic?" *Today's Christian Woman* magazine

NO love of the natural heart is safe unless the human heart has been satisfied by God first.

Oswald Chambers
The Best from All His Books

In the Beginning

IF you are considering marriage, ask yourself one question: Will I still enjoy talking with her when I'm old?

Friedrich Nietzsche
Human, All Too Human

$\mathcal{A}$ MAN when he is making up to anybody can be cordial and gallant and full of little attentions and altogether charming. But when a man is really in love, he can't help looking like a sheep.

Agatha Christie
The Mystery of the Blue Train

$\mathcal{I}$F couples would put half the effort into marriage that they put into courtship, they would be surprised how things will brighten up.

Billy Graham
"My Answer," syndicated newspaper column

$\mathcal{T}$HERE'S a story about a young couple who decided to start their honeymoon by kneeling beside their bed to pray. The bride giggled when she heard her new husband's prayer: "For what we are about to receive, may the Lord make us truly thankful."

Les and Leslie Parrott
"Skimming the Surface?" *Marriage Partnership* magazine

Expectations

*E*VERY love relationship is based on unwritten conventions rashly agreed upon by the lovers during the first weeks of their love. On the one hand, they are living a sort of dream; on the other hand, without realizing it, they are drawing up the fine print of their contracts like the most hard-nosed lawyers. O lovers! Be wary during those perilous first days! If you serve the other party breakfast in bed, you will be obliged to continue same in perpetuity or face charges of animosity and treason!

Milan Kundera
The Book of Laughter and Forgetting

$\mathcal{M}$ARRIAGE—as its veterans know well—is the continuous process of getting used to things you hadn't expected.

Tom Mullen
in *Speaker's Sourcebook II*

$\mathcal{I}$ WAS in love with her but wasn't at all sure she was the girl I should ask to marry me. My plan was to marry a perfect person who had no peers, someone everyone could recognize as an angel. Whenever I was attracted to a girl on campus, I began to run through a mental inventory, analyzing that girl's good points as compared to Margaret's. I could always find excellent qualities that I thought Margaret lacked, and my mind was in a whirl. . . .

I discussed my problem with a friend, a senior big-man-on-campus type. His response was brusque: "Look, if you *could* find a perfect girl, she wouldn't marry *you!*"

Ken Taylor
My Life: A Guided Tour

*D*EAR Abby: I am forty-four and would like to meet a man my age with no bad habits. —Rose

```
Dear Rose: So would I.
```

Abigail Van Buren
"Dear Abby," syndicated newspaper column

*K*EEP your eyes open before marriage, half shut afterwards.

Benjamin Franklin
Maxims and Morals

*J*UST as a hungry tick clamps on to a nourishing host in anticipation of a meal, so each partner unites with the other in the expectation of finding what his or her personal nature demands. The rather frustrating dilemma, of course, is that in such a marriage there are two ticks and no dog.

Larry Crabb
How to Become One with Your Mate

*B*EFORE marriage, each by instinct strives to be what the other wants. The young woman desires to look sexy and takes up interest in sports. The young man notices plants and flowers, and works at asking questions instead of just answering monosyllabically. After marriage, the process slows and somewhat reverses. Each insists on his or her rights. Each resists bending to the other's will. After years, though, that process may subtly begin to reverse again. I sense a new willingness to bend back toward what the other wants, maturely this time, not out of a desire to catch a mate but out of a desire to please a mate who shared a quarter-century of life.

Philip Yancey
"My Legs Ache, but We Made It," *Christianity Today* magazine

I HAVE great hopes that we shall love each other all our lives as much as if we had never married at all.

Lord Byron
in a letter to Annabella Milbanke

THE great truth is that women actually like men, and men can never believe it.

Isabel Patterson
in *The Romance Factor*

Who'd

I Marry, Anyway?

*I*F you want to sacrifice the admiration of many men for the criticism of one, go ahead, get married.

Katherine Hepburn
in *A Remarkable Woman*

IN most marriages, husbands and wives eventually adapt to each other's differences, no matter how eccentric they are. One of the things I've had to adapt to is that Bill is very frugal (tight is the word!). For instance, sometime back when my publisher notified us that sales of my books had reached the one million mark, Bill said we ought to celebrate. He got in the car and disappeared for a while, and I imagined him arranging some quiet little dinner party at a fancy restaurant or even shopping for some special gift for me. Jewelry would be nice, I thought. Instead he came home, smiling broadly, with two bunches of fresh asparagus! "I know how much you love it," he said as he dropped his gift into the kitchen sink. . . . Hardly *my* way of celebrating!

Barbara Johnson
I'm So Glad You Told Me What I Didn't Wanna Hear

I AM not at all the sort of person you and I took me for.

Jane Carlyle
in a letter to Thomas Carlyle

SUCCESS in marriage depends on being able, when you get over being in love, to really love. . . . You never know anyone until you marry them.

Eleanor Roosevelt
My Day

WHEN true love comes, that which is counterfeit will be recognized. For someday, it will rain on the picnic, ants will sting, mosquitos will bite, and you will get indigestion from the potato salad. There will be no stars in your eyes, no sunsets on your horizon. Love will be black and white with no piped-in music. But you will say "forever," because love is a choice you have made.

Ruth Senter
"Say 'Forever'," *Marriage Partnership* magazine

NEVER, never did we marry just the piece of a human being—even though it's only bits and pieces we see before the marriage. We marry the other one whole. But always we buy the package before we can open it.

Walter Wangerin Jr.
As for Me and My House

COMMITMENT to marriage also requires courage when your mate doesn't change.

Diane Eble
"Marriage Ain't for Wimps," *Marriage Partnership* magazine

BY all means marry; if you get a good wife, you'll become happy; if you get a bad one, you'll become a philosopher.

Socrates

THE honeymoon is over when he phones that he'll be late for supper—and she has already left a note that it's in the refrigerator.

Bill Lawrence
in *Peter's Quotations* (Laurence J. Peter, ed.)

ON Friday, October 15, 1948, just a little more than two weeks before the general congressional election, Betty and I were married. I had been campaigning until minutes before the ceremony and when I walked up to the altar, I had mud on my shoes. My mother was furious, but Betty pretended not to notice, and friends still kid me about it to this day. Our honeymoon was brief. After we returned to Grand Rapids late the following Monday afternoon, I told Betty that I wouldn't be home for dinner that night. "Can you make me a sandwich?" I asked. "There's a meeting tonight I just have to attend." . . . That was her introduction to married life.

Gerald Ford
A Time to Heal

What Is Marriage?

IF you move a train east from Des Moines toward Chicago, two changes have to happen. You become closer to Chicago but farther away from Des Moines. You cannot become closer to Chicago and remain close to Des Moines at the same time. The same fact exists in marriage. An intimate relationship with my new partner will change the close relationships with my old friends.

William Coleman
Engaged

$\mathcal{T}$HE meaning of marriage begins in the giving of words. We cannot join ourselves to one another without giving our word. And this must be an unconditional giving, for in joining ourselves to one another we join ourselves to the unknown. . . . You do not know the road; you have committed your life to a way.

Ralph Waldo Emerson

$\mathcal{A}$ SUCCESSFUL marriage is one in which you fall in love many times, always with the same person.

D. W. McLaughlin
in Practical Proverbs & Wacky Wit

$\mathcal{T}$O have and to hold from this day forward, for better for worse, for richer for poorer, in sickness and in health, to love and to cherish, till death do us part.

Book of Common Prayer

$\mathcal{M}$ARRIAGE is not simply the luck of the draw, or something that we get involved in which just unfolds before us like a long movie. Good marriages, like good individual lives or good art, are conscious creations. They are made.

Kevin and Marilyn Ryan

Making a Marriage

$\mathcal{T}$HERE is no relationship between human beings so close as that of husband and wife, if they are united as they ought to be. . . . The power of this love is truly stronger than any passion; other desires may be strong, but this one alone never fades. . . . Can you see now how close this union is, and how God providentially created it from a single nature? . . . God caused the entire human race to proceed from this one point of origin. He did not, on the one hand, fashion woman independently from man; otherwise man would think of her as essentially different from himself. Nor did He enable woman to bear children without man; if this were the case she would be self-sufficient. . . . He made it impossible for men and women to be self-sufficient.

St. John Chrysostom

$\mathcal{M}$ARRIAGE is to human relations what mono-theism is to theology. It is a decision to put all the eggs in one basket, to go for broke, to bet all of the marbles.

Mike Mason
The Mystery of Marriage

$\mathcal{M}$ARRIAGE is the only adventure open to the cowardly.

Voltaire
Penseés d'un Philosphe

$\mathcal{V}$OLTAIRE thought marriage was the only adventure open to cowards. But Voltaire never married, or he would have known that marriage requires a greal deal of courage.

Hubert Downs
in *Journey out of Prague*

$\mathcal{A}$S God by creation made two of one, so again by marriage he made one of two.

Thomas Adams
in *Gathered Gold*

FOR each of the partners, getting married involves a rupture with his or her former reality and the construction of a new, private sphere which is the special turf of the two people involved.

Maggie Scarf
Intimate Partners: Patterns in Love and Marriage

THE best marriages, like the best lives, were both happy and unhappy. There was even a kind of necessary tension, a certain tautness between the partners that gave the marriage strength, like the tautness of a full sail.

Anne Morrow Lindbergh
Dearly Beloved

IN an enduring and happy marriage, there is a commitment both to the spouse and to the institution of marriage.

Jeanette and Robert Lauer
'Til Death Do Us Part

MARRIAGE is one long conversation, chequered by disputes.

Robert Louis Stevenson
Memories and Portraits

$\mathcal{T}$HE Puritans called marriage "the little church within the church." In marriage, every day you love, and every day you forgive. It is an ongoing sacrament—love and forgiveness.

Bill Moyers
in *The Power of Myth*

$\mathcal{W}$E complement each other very well. For example, if I need to know how to spell something, I can ask Mavis; if the toilet breaks she can ask me.

Jay Leno
in *Us* magazine

$\mathcal{A}$ MARRIAGE in which each person brings ideas, attitudes and approaches—even to the point of creating disagreements—is a marriage that will build on the best that both partners have to offer.

Neil Clark Warren
"Work It Out," *Focus on the Family* magazine

$\mathcal{W}$HILE my children were growing up and at the age where they were beginning the dating process, I would sometimes ask them about a certain person of the opposite sex whose name would surface. "She is just a good friend, Dad," they would reply. I sometimes remarked to them that a good friendship is a strong basis for a good marriage. Obviously they rolled their eyes, since marriage was the last thing on their minds at the time. Your spouse should be your best friend, and if he or she is not, you need to discover a renewed relationship that involves more than sharing sex, kids, and the checkbook.

Bill Carmichael

*L*IFE is war, and marriage provides us with a close and intimate ally with whom we may wage this war.

Dan B. Allender and Tremper Longman
Intimate Allies

*T*HERE'S something really great about waking up and knowing somebody loves you and that you love somebody. I know that sounds gooey, but it's true. Plus you always have a date for New Year's Eve.

Billy Crystal
in *Marriage Partnership* magazine

The Marriage
Journey

BESIDES being a great way to exercise, walking together reminds us [that] marriage is a journey, not a destination. It's a marathon, not a sprint. It's a lifetime union of two imperfect people who love each other.

Claudia Arp
"Is Your Spouse Driving You Nuts?" *Today's Christian Woman* magazine

IF marriage is a journey, as I've heard it said, then God must be a master at sign posting. Marriage is his idea, after all, and his destination for wives and husbands remains fixed: oneness of body, oneness of soul (Ephesians 5:31). It seems reasonable that a loving Father would post signs to direct those of us who want to stay on course.

Paul Kortepeter
"Ridin' on the Freeway of Love," *Marriage Partnership* magazine

BUT Ruth replied, "Don't ask me to leave you and turn back. I will go wherever you go and live wherever you live. Your people will be my people, and your God will be my God. I will die where you die and will be buried there. May the Lord punish me severely if I allow anything but death to separate us!"

Ruth 1:16-17

SO many couples destroy each other because they are afraid to give up their right to be right.

David Stoop
Seeking God Together

*M*ARRIAGE doesn't just happen! It takes a solid set of decisions, a huge amount of skill and enormous willpower.

Neil Clark Warren
The Triumphant Marriage

*T*HE encounter in love is an encounter without weapons. . . . We are very able to hide our guns and knives even in the most intimate relationship. An old bitter memory, a slight suspicion about motives, or a small doubt can be as sharp as a knife held behind our back as a weapon for defense in case of attack. . . . Table and bed are the two places of intimacy where love can manifest itself in weakness. In love men and women take off all forms of power, embracing each other in total disarmament. The nakedness of their body is only a symbol of total vulnerability and availability.

Henri J. M. Nouwen
Intimacy

*T*RUST us: One day your kids will grow up and leave home. That's why it's so important to find mutual enjoyment in each other's interests and hobbies now.

Dave and Claudia Arp
"Four Steps toward Each Other," *Virtue* magazine

*I*T is said in marriage, the man and woman give each other "his or her nethermost beast" to hold. Each holds the leash for the "nethermost beast" of the other.

Robert Bly
Iron John

*I*F two people who have been strangers, as all of us are, suddenly let the wall between them break down and feel close, feel one, this moment of oneness is one of the most exhilarating, most exciting, experiences in life.

Erich Fromm
The Art of Loving

*I*T is impossible for two human beings to be one while scrupulously respecting the distance that separates them, unless God is present in each of them. The point where parallels meet is infinity.

Simone Weil
in *Into the Garden: A Wedding Anthology*

*C*OUPLES who frequently pray together are twice as likely as those who pray less often to describe their marriages as being highly romantic. And get this—married couples who pray together are 90 percent more likely to report higher satisfaction with their sex lives than couples who don't pray together. Prayer, because of the vulnerability it demands, also draws a couple closer.

Les and Leslie Parrott
"Skimming the Surface?" *Marriage Partnership* magazine

THE weaving of lives is really the interpenetrating of stories that not only give us a glimpse of each other and ourselves but also offer a taste of the mystery of God's work in human relationships.

Dan B. Allender and Tremper Longman
Intimate Allies

THE early glow gives way . . . to a growing sense of companionship, mutuality, a striving toward a common goal, deepening understanding and respect for each other. [It may take] five, ten, or twenty years working out a satisfying relationship: giving and forgiving, growing, maturing, learning to accept anger as not incompatible with love.

Cecil Osborne
The Art of Understanding Your Mate

$\mathcal{M}$ARRIAGE is a continuous process and not a static condition. It is a plant and not a piece of furniture.

Harold Nicolson
in Speaking of Marriage

$\mathcal{T}$HE survival of love depends on the management of change.

Ari Kiev
How to Keep Love Alive

$\mathcal{A}$LL love relationships are something of a dance in which two people are constantly moving, sometimes coming close together and again moving away to gain some space. Occasionally, they may find themselves far apart, but that does not mean the dance is over. If they are patient and do not bolt, they can draw close together again.

Alan Loy McGinnis
The Romance Factor

$\mathcal{L}$ife isn't like a book. Life isn't logical or sensible or orderly. Life is a mess most of the

time. And theology must be lived in the midst
of that mess.

Charles Colson
in *Quotable Quotations* (Lloyd Cory, ed.)

*L*IFE is seasonal. So are relationships. They
have inevitable ebbs and flows. Since life is a
journey, the scenery is constantly changing.
Recognizing the inevitable "lulls" of relationships
is one thing. Resigning ourselves to them, however,
would be a mistake.

Brett Selby
"When There Is a Lull," *Home Life* magazine

*W*ITHIN the context of a committed marriage,
life with its demands can at times drain romance
from a man and woman. But love can be renewed
and refreshed in a marriage where the broader
idea of intimacy, of vulnerable trust, is there.

Bill and Nancie Carmichael

*M*ARRIAGE, even under the very best of
circumstances, is a crisis . . . and it is a dangerous
thing not to be aware of this. Whether it turns out
to be a healthy, challenging, and constructive crisis
or a disastrous nightmare depends largely upon

how willing the partners are to be changed. . . . Yet
ironically, it is some of the most hardened and
crusty and unlikely people in the world who
plunge themselves into the arms of marriage and
thereby submit in almost total naivete to the two
most transforming powers known to the human
heart: the love of another person and the gracious
love of God.

Mike Mason
The Mystery of Marriage

Two

Are Better than One

*T*WO people can accomplish more than twice as much as one. . . . If one person falls, the other can reach out and help. . . . A person standing alone can be attacked and defeated, but two can stand back-to-back and conquer. Three are even better, for a triple-braided cord is not easily broken.

Ecclesiates 4:9-10, 12

$\mathcal{S}$LOWLY, awkwardly, with tears streaming down our faces, we reluctantly reached out to one another. Neither of us knew how much strength we had to give, but we were willing to share it. We gave one another something that most friendships are not able to give— vulnerability. Throughout our years together, we had built up a history and a closeness so subtle even we didn't know it was there. On that evening, we admitted we couldn't handle life alone. We needed one another.

Erma Bombeck
A Marriage Made in Heaven or Too Tired for an Affair

"$\mathcal{A}$T last!" Adam exclaimed. "She is part of my own flesh and bone!" . . . This explains why a man leaves his father and mother and is joined to his wife, and the two are united into one.

Genesis 2:23-24

$\mathcal{C}$ARE and consistency are point and counter- point in the music of marriage. They are played in a delicate dust of mutual need. And we have got to be forever improvising on the score of who cares for whom and who is cared for at any given moment of need. Each of the players trusts the other to move in to take up the slack when one of them misses a beat.

Lewis B. Smedes
Caring and Commitment

$\mathcal{G}$RIEF can take care of itself; but to get the full value of joy you must have someone to divide it with.

Mark Twain
Wit and Wisecracks

$\mathcal{T}$HE goal of marriage is two-fold: to reveal the glory of God and to enhance the glory of one's spouse.

Dan B. Allender and Tremper Longman
Intimate Allies

$\mathcal{W}$HEN you reach out as a team, something good happens—an almost mystical bonding of husband and wife. Reaching out promotes humility, sharing, compassion and intimacy. Doing good for others helps couples transcend themselves and become part of something larger.

Les and Leslie Parrott
"Skimming the Surface?" *Marriage Partnership* magazine

*T*HE man who finds a wife finds a treasure and receives favor from the Lord.

Proverbs 18:22

*T*HE most precious gift that marriage gave was this constant impact of something very close and intimate yet all the time. . . . No cranny of heart or body remained unsatisfied.

C. S. Lewis
in C. S. Lewis through the Shadowlands

*Y*OU are like a private garden, my treasure, my bride! You are like a spring that no one else can drink from, a fountain of my own.

Song of Songs 4:12

*T*HE camaraderie of best friends who are also lovers seems twice as exciting and doubly precious.

Ed Wheat
Love Life for Every Married Couple

The Meaning
of

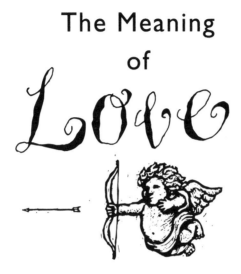

$\mathcal{I}$F a man really loves a woman, of course he wouldn't marry her for the world if he were not quite sure that he was the best person she could by any possibility marry.

Oliver Wendell Holmes
The Autocrat of the Breakfast-Table

LOVE never fails. Money, youth, and motor-
boats all fail. Waistlines stretch, teeth vanish,
eyes weaken. Skin wrinkles, heads bald, arches
drop. Love and love alone never gives up.

William Coleman
Engaged

MARITAL love demands courage because
spouses are required to set aside personal needs
and serve another person, with no assurance that
their own needs will be met.

Diane Eble
"Marriage Ain't for Wimps," *Marriage Partnership* magazine

I DON'T exist to like, but I do exist to love.
Contrary to liking, love demands nothing in
return.

Hugh Prather
Notes to Myself

LOVE does not consist in gazing at each other
but in looking outward together in the same
direction.

Antoine de Saint-Exupéry

*L*OVE seems the swiftest, but it is the slowest of all growths. No man or woman really knows what perfect love is until they have been married a quarter of a century.

Mark Twain

*L*OVE must be learned, and learned again and again; there is no end to it. Hate needs no instruction, but waits only to be provoked.

Katherine Anne Porter
in *The Marriage Affair*

*I*F human love does not carry a man beyond himself, it is not love. If love is always discreet, always wise, always sensible and calculating, never carried beyond itself, it is not love at all. It may be affection, it may be warmth of feeling, but it has not the true nature of love in it.

Oswald Chambers
My Utmost for His Highest

*L*OVE never gives up, never loses faith, is always hopeful, and endures through every circumstance.

1 Corinthians 13:7

The Art of *Loving*

ℛOMANCE was never my strong suit. I proposed to [my wife] Lynne in her parents' garage; I took my Harley-Davidson on our honeymoon; I thought our best anniversary was the one we spent watching a video of *Rocky III*. But several years into our marriage, I realized that being a godly husband meant more than bringing home a paycheck and occasionally talking shop with Lynne. I had to grow in the gentle art of romance.

Bill and Lynne Hybels
Fit to Be Tied

ONCE you marry, you're not to stop all the attentive responses. They're to increase. It's a continual attitude. Keeping the romance alive is a matter of little daily acts. It means that your spouse is on your mind, not just: "Oh no, it's Valentine's Day again. I better go buy something and do something romantic."

H. Norman Wright
"The Wright Stuff," *Virtue* magazine

MORE romance in your marriage may depend on your choice to accept and treasure your husband for who he is. If he doesn't sense acceptance and feels you're pushing him to change, he may become more resistant. Your husband needs to feel love unconditionally.

Jean Lush
"Isn't It Romantic?" *Today's Christian Woman* magazine

MARRIED life . . . isn't a time for settling down but for growth, for doing new things. With each passing year a growing couple will actively look for new and different things they can do together.

Dale Evans Rogers
God in the Hard Times

$\mathcal{A}$ WOMAN who knows that inside every man, no matter how old, how successful, or how powerful, there is a little boy who wants to be loved and to feel as if he's special, is a woman who knows a powerful secret.

Ellen Kreidman
Light His Fire: How to Keep Your Man Passionately and Hopelessly in Love with You

$\mathcal{I}$F you have needs which are unmet, instead of making demands or accusations, try to meet the needs of your marriage partner. Love begets love; resentment begets hostility; rejection begets rejection.

Cecil Osborne
The Art of Understanding Your Mate

$\mathcal{H}$OW do I love thee? Let me count the ways. I love thee to the depth and breadth and height My soul can reach.

Elizabeth Barrett Browning
Sonnets from the Portuguese

$\mathcal{T}$OMORROW morning, get your eyes off the toast . . . long enough to LOOK at your spouse. . . . Look at his or her hands. Do you remember when just to look at those hands made your heart lift? Well, LOOK . . . and remember. Then loose your tongue and tell him or her how you feel. . . . Ask the Lord to give you a sentimental, romantic, physical, in-love kind of love for your spouse. God will do this. His love in us can change the actual physical quality of our love for our spouses.

Ed Wheat
Love Life for Every Married Couple

$\mathcal{G}$RUMBLING is the death of love.

Marlene Dietrich
Marlene Dietrich's ABC

$\mathcal{A}$ HEALTHY [sexual] relationship is one in which the two partners are engaged in the ongoing process of attracting and luring one another to bed.

Andrew Greeley
Sexual Intimacy

*P*LACE me like a seal over your heart, or like a seal on your arm. For love is as strong as death, and its jealousy is as enduring as the grave. Love flashes like fire, the brightest kind of flame. Many waters cannot quench love; neither can rivers drown it. If a man tried to buy love with everything he owned, his offer would be utterly despised.

Song of Songs 8:6-7

*T*O view our spouses from the lens of glory is to be overwhelmed by the privilege of being face-to-face with a creature who mirrors God.

Dan B. Allender and Tremper Longman
Intimate Allies

*T*HERE is an old story about a man who gave a simple formula for a long and happy marriage: "I always treated her in a way that meant she couldn't replace me with a hot-water bottle when I died."

Jeanette and Robert Lauer
'Til Death Do Us Part

$\mathcal{W}$E heard a true story from a recent participant in a seminar who tried to apply the concept of meaningful touching with his wife, and it left him in an embarrassing situation!

After hearing the concept of meaningful touching talked about over and over, it really stuck with this man. One afternoon after cutting the grass, he came in to take a shower and clean up. He had left the bedroom door open, and when he finished his shower he walked to the rack to get a towel. From where he stood, he could see his wife standing in the kitchen preparing their dinner.

What a time for meaningful touching, he thought to himself. Without a moment's thought, he ran down the hall in his birthday suit and burst into the kitchen to give his wife a big hug. What he couldn't see from the bedroom or as he raced down the hall was his neighbor's wife, who had come over to visit. That shocked neighbor saw a great deal more of this husband than she had ever expected! His timing was terrible, but no one could fault his commitment to meaningfully touch his wife!

Gary Smalley and John Trent
The Blessing

How Do I Say
I Love you?

LISTENING to my spouse is one of the most significant ways to say "I love you." All too often I listen with the intent to reply, or I allow my presence to be there, but my thoughts are tuned elsewhere, or my mind has already formed some opinion, or I think my spouse wants an answer that includes solutions. But I find that often, the only thing my spouse really needs is to feel heard and understood.

Bill and Nancie Carmichael

*T*HEY do not love who do not show their love.

William Shakespeare

*E*VEN as a kid, I could tell they were different from other kids' parents. For instance, my dad was not one to go off golfing or bowling with the guys. He preferred to be with my mother. And my mother wouldn't roll her eyes and make jokes at my father's expense when he wasn't around, as other mothers in the neighborhood did. Instead my mother would say: "You know, he has never disappointed me, not once."

Jeanne Marie Laskas
"I Send You a Cream-White Rosebud . . ." *Florida Magazine*

*H*OW sweet is your love, my treasure, my bride! How much better it is than wine! Your perfume is more fragrant than the richest of spices. Your lips, my bride, are as sweet as honey. Yes, honey and cream are under your tongue. The scent of your clothing is like that of the mountains and the cedars of Lebanon.

Song of Songs 4:10-11

USE humor with care. Never try to be funny by criticizing your spouse. . . . Questions to ask before using humor are "Will this increase tension or relieve it?"; "Can I laugh at myself, or am I just trying to poke fun at my mate?"; "Am I trying to win points for my side with cute remarks?"

H. Norman Wright
Communication: Key to Your Marriage

NEVER try to guess your wife's size. Just buy her anything marked "petite" and hold on to the receipt.

Barbara Johnson
Splashes of Joy in the Cesspools of Life

A LOVER . . . provides delight, but he also protects, provides care, and helps to avoid discouragement, weariness, boredom.

Andrew Greeley
Sexual Intimacy

AND you husbands must love your wives with the same love Christ showed the church. He gave up his life for her.

Ephesians 5:25

*I*T'S true, he's never given me jewelry, red roses or a box of chocolates for any holiday, but does that necessarily mean the guy doesn't have a heart, or that he doesn't love me? Maybe all it means is that we don't speak the same language when it comes to love.

Nancy Kennedy
Steel-Belted, Radical Love

*O*N Christmas Day, [my wife] Diane's last present for me was only a little envelope. But inside was a savings account passbook, in which were recorded little deposits she had been making secretly all year: $7.50 here, $5.00 there, she squirreled away from her paycheck. Without my knowing, she had been saving all year to give me a ski trip for Christmas, and when she handed me the passbook, the account had added up to $1,200.

So in January we left our furniture-free living room behind and had a glorious ten days in Utah. We ate shrimp until we couldn't walk, we skied in the powdered snow, we drove to Salt Lake City to hear the Mormon Tabernacle Choir rehearse one cold night. We laughed and made love and absorbed together all the beauties there were to see in one week.

The furniture for the living room could come

later, and it did, but opportunities to witness each other's joy at a fresh snowstorm would never come again in just that fashion. During that week, I thought about all those months of Diane's planning for this—the lunches she'd skipped, the sales she'd passed up. Here was the thing that meant most: She had occupied many scattered moments during the year scheming and planning for something she knew would make me happy. One never forgets such acts of kindness; they help build up a friendship, like many layers of fine lacquer finish.

Alan Loy McGinnis
The Romance Factor

Be an Encourager

$\mathcal{E}$XPRESS appreciation for each other.
Accepting each other makes a stable marriage.
Appreciating each other, however, makes a
sensational marriage.

Brett Selby
"When There Is a Lull," *Home Life* magazine

$\mathcal{H}$USBAND, your wife needs to know that you see her as she is and think that she is beautiful—inside and out. This will actually produce a shining new loveliness to delight you. Wives who believe they are beautiful *are* beautiful.

As one wife told us, "This week I was really down. I'm struggling to lose fifteen pounds, and I hate my new haircut, and I have a cold. I'm tired and my eyes are red, and I feel like I can't do anything right. Do you know what my husband did? He put his arms around me, looked at me very deeply, very searchingly, and then he said, 'I find you altogether lovely.' The way he said it, I knew he meant it. I honestly believe that moment changed my whole life. I'll never forget it!"

Ed Wheat
The First Years of Forever

$\mathcal{I}$N marriage, each partner is to be an encourager rather than a critic, a forgiver rather than a collector of hurts, an enabler rather than a reformer.

H. Norman Wright and Gary J. Oliver
How to Change Your Spouse (Without Ruining Your Marriage)

_I_ THINK sometimes the reason husbands aren't more involved at home is because we ask them to do something and then we get upset when they don't do it our way. And when we interfere, we undermine the very thing we've asked them to do and be.

Karen Mains
Parenting: Questions Women Ask

_O_NE of the highest functions of a wife is to console her husband for all the blows he receives in life. Yet, in order to console, there is no need to say very much. It is enough to listen, to understand, to love. Look at that mother whose child runs crying to her knees. She utters no word, and yet in a moment the tears have disappeared, the child jumps down, smiles all over his face, and heads out into the world once more where he will receive new blows. In every man, even the most eminent and the apparently strongest, there remains something of the child who needs to be consoled.

Paul Tournier
To Understand Each Other

$\textit{M}$YTH: It's not good to show too much gratitude.

"If I said thank you all the time to my wife it would sound phony," one husband told me. "By not saying it all the time, it means more to her when I finally do say it."

This man was dead wrong. Expressing gratitude is a form of love, and you can never show too much love. If your rare compliments are well-received, that doesn't necessarily mean your spouse feels more appreciated. She may simply feel relieved that she isn't as unappreciated as she was beginning to believe.

Paul Coleman
"Myths about the Magical Word 'Thanks',"
Marriage Partnership magazine

$\textit{W}$E often withhold expressions of admiration and thankfulness from those closest to us. The story is told of a taciturn gentleman in Vermont who eventually said to his wife, "When I think of how much you have meant to me all these years, it is almost more than I can do sometimes to keep from telling you so."

Jack and Carole Mayhall
Marriage Takes More Than Love

Be a Servant

*T*HE more emotionally mature we are, the fewer demands we make upon others, and the more capable we are of being concerned about others and their needs.

Cecil Osborne
The Art of Understanding Your Mate

$\mathcal{T}$HE husband should not deprive his wife of sexual intimacy, which is her right as a married woman, nor should the wife deprive her husband. The wife gives authority over her body to her husband, and the husband also gives authority over his body to his wife. So do not deprive each other of sexual relations. The only exception to this rule would be the agreement of both husband and wife.

1 Corinthians 7:3-5

$\mathcal{M}$UTUAL submission is the only workable path to a strong marriage. . . . Submission is not obeying another; it is putting oneself under the other to serve the good of God for that person's life.

Dan B. Allender and Tremper Longman
Intimate Allies

Be an

$\mathcal{S}$TAND up for your husband. We learn in Proverbs that "A friend loveth at all times, and a brother is born for adversity" (Proverbs 17:17, KJV). When you are your husband's best friend, you believe in him no matter what happens. This often means going to "bat" for him when job trials overwhelm him or telling other family members of the good qualities of your husband.

Some marriage partners only pretend to be friends. Yet where there is a true friendship in a marriage, a spouse doesn't hesitate in sticking up for the other.

Bob and Debbie Bruce
"20 Inexpensive Ways to Say 'I Love You'," *Home Life* magazine

ONE of the most empowering qualities of good marriages is trust. To trust someone also means to trust their judgment in making good decisions. Some people don't trust their mate with the checkbook, some constantly attack their spouse's daily decisions, some fight constantly over trivial things like who's right about the shortest route to a friend's house. Some who are emotionally insecure incessantly challenge their spouse with a do-you-really-love-me question. All of these have to do with trust. Good relationships have trust as a cornerstone.

Bill and Nancie Carmichael

IT seems a teacher, on the first day of class, was given a list of the children's names; each name was followed by a two- or three-digit number. At the end of the course, the children's grades coincided with the numbers the teacher had been given. The student with 140 after his name received an A while the student with 87 after his name received an F. Only after marking grades did the teacher find out that those original numbers were not IQ scores but locker numbers. The teacher had made assumptions about the students' abilities, and they all lived up (or down) to those expectations. In teaming up, you ought to assume the highest score possible for your mate.

Albert and Carol Allman Lee
The Total Couple

*E*STIMATE her by the qualities she has, and not by the qualities she may not have. This is marriage.

Charles Dickens

The Art of
Communication

COMMUNICATION between two human beings can be confusing, especially if one is the husband and the other is the wife.

Mack and Brenda Timberlake
Lifesavers for Your Marriage

$\mathcal{T}$RUE intimacy . . . exists in marriage when each feels free to share innermost feelings with the other, knowing that the sharing of those feelings will not lessen the other's commitment to love.

Nancie Carmichael
My Husband, My Friend

$\mathcal{T}$HE point of marriage is not to create a quick commonality by tearing down all boundaries; on the contrary, a good marriage is one in which each partner appoints the other to be the guardian of his solitude, and thus they show each other the greatest possible trust.

Robert Hass and Stephen Miller
Into the Garden: A Wedding Anthology

$\mathcal{I}$NTIMACY can grow only in a place of safety. When husband and wife are afraid of hurt, rebuff, criticism, and misunderstanding, they will find it difficult to touch and share freely. . . . If you want real intimacy in your marriage, you will have to establish trust in your relationship.

Ed Wheat
Love Life for Every Married Couple

*E*ACH member of the couple must be aware of what is going on in the mind of the other. You don't do that with most people in your life. You don't need to—many personal things you just keep to yourself. But in a relationship as close as marriage, you are living a shared life; and if you don't know what the other person is feeling, thinking, and planning, you'll soon be in trouble.

David and Vera Mace
Three Essentials for a Successful Marriage

*H*OW we talk to each other reflects the quality of our relationship as well as the depth of our character.

Dan B. Allender and Tremper Longman
Intimate Allies

*O*FTEN the difference between a successful marriage and a mediocre one consists of leaving about three or four things a day unsaid.

Harlan Miller
in *Peter's Quotations* (Laurence J. Peter, ed.)

$\mathcal{T}$RUTHFULNESS means that, when you talk, you make a most careful bridge of your words. This requires two cares, really: care for the topic, to get it right; and care for your spouse, that she or he hears it right.

Walter Wangerin Jr.
As for Me and My House

$\mathcal{S}$PEAK when you're angry, and you'll deliver the best speech you'll ever regret.
Adapted from *Dynamic Preaching* (November 1987)

$\mathcal{I}$T is easy to fly into a passion—anybody can do that—but to be angry with the right person to the right extent and at the right time and with the right object and in the right way—that is not easy.

Aristotle

$\mathcal{S}$OME people use the "silent treatment" as a means of avoiding controversy. They use silence as a weapon to control, frustrate or manipulate their spouse. Or sometimes the husband and wife take the pathway of silence because it seems to be the least painful. . . . But silence never pays off in the long run. "Silence is golden" so the saying goes, but it can also be yellow! Don't hide behind silence because you are afraid to deal with the issue at hand.

H. Norman Wright
Communication: Key to Your Marriage

*I*F I ignore the emotional plea and respond only to the words, I will not be communicating with you. The heart of any conversation is the demand being made on my emotions. If I feel frustrated, that is a good sign I am avoiding the emotions you are trying to communicate—I have not paused long enough to ask, "What do you really want from me?"

Hugh Prather
Notes to Myself

*M*ARRIAGE might be called the capacity to finish one another's sentences. I suspect it succeeds to the degree that this capacity fails.

Amanda Cross
No Word from Winifred

*I*T is easy to think that you know what your partner is going to say, so you cut your partner off and finish the sentence or interrupt his idea with something that he or she doesn't mean at all. All too often a husband or wife blurts out an opinion that is miles from the wavelength that the other partner is on. The writer of Proverbs said: "What a shame—yes, how stupid!—to decide before knowing the facts!" (Proverbs 18:13, TLB)

H. Norman Wright
Communication: Key to Your Marriage

WE pay attention only long enough to develop a counter-argument; we critique [their] ideas; we mentally grade and pigeon-hole each other. . . . People often listen with an agenda, to sell, or petition, or seduce. Seldom is there a deep, open-hearted, unjudging reception of the other. . . . By contrast, if someone truly listens to me, my spirit begins to expand.

Mary Rose O'Reilley
"Deep Listening: An Experimental Friendship," *Weavings* magazine

IT is impossible to overemphasize the immense need humans have to be really listened to, to be taken seriously, to be understood. No one can develop freely in this world and find a full life without feeling understood by at least one person. . . . Listen to couples. They are for the most part dialogues of the deaf.

Paul Tournier
To Understand Each Other

To listen to someone means I see you . . . I am here for you . . . I am feeling what you feel. Maybe with no answers, but I'm here. I think Winnie-the-Pooh sums up this idea best. One day Winnie-the-Pooh and Piglet were walking along together. Pooh sidled up to Piglet and put his paw in Piglet's. "What?" said Piglet. "Oh nothing," said Pooh, "I just want to be sure of you."

Bill and Nancie Carmichael

Two ways I have of talking "at" the other person instead of "with" him are: talking in order to seduce him into thinking I am right, and talking in order to sound right to myself.

Hugh Prather
Notes to Myself

The Art of Compromise

$\mathcal{M}$ARRIED love is hard work, because it requires us to constantly think of our spouse instead of ourself, and our natural bent is to think of ourself first.

Bill and Nancie Carmichael

$\mathcal{P}$EOPLE who establish successful loving unions do so by letting the other person be a whole person, rather than forcing him or her to be only one-half of a whole.

Ari Kiev
How to Keep Love Alive

$\mathcal{W}$HATEVER change you seek needs to be advantageous for both you and your partner, as well as for the relationship. It's not our responsibility to take on the job of reformer. The Holy Spirit can do that much better than we can. Our task is to request change with our spouse and provide an atmosphere of acceptance and patience that allows God freedom to work. Then we must learn to trust God to do the work.

H. Norman Wright and Gary J. Oliver
How to Change Your Spouse (Without Ruining Your Marriage)

$\mathcal{A}$ RELATIONSHIP doesn't need both of its partners if they are exactly the same. The wonderful thing you do for your marriage is to share that part of you that is different from your mate. But as sure as you do share your differences, there is bound to be conflict. This is the kind of healthy conflict, though, that gives you the opportunity to expand your marriage.

Neil Clark Warren
"Work It Out," *Focus on the Family* magazine

$\mathcal{W}$HEN a man and a woman marry, they become one. Of course, they must decide which one, and that is often where the storm starts.

Pierce Harris
in *Braude's Second Encyclopedia of Stories, Quotations and Anecdotes*

$\mathcal{L}$EARNING to share control—to submit to one another in marriage—is a process. If we're ready to delegate responsibility to each other according to our unique abilities, control issues will become less dominant. And when there is conflict, remember that it can actually be good for your marriage. . . . Conflict is a getaway to intimacy because it pushes us to grow and to share the truth about ourselves.

Eileen Silva Kindig
"Who's the Boss?" *Marriage Partnership* magazine

$\mathcal{A}$ COUPLE must find out for themselves where the various "spheres of influence" lie: who pays the bills, who casts the deciding vote on buying what house, renting which apartment, where to vacation. A selfish husband or wife may insist on rendering a final verdict on all decisions, major and minor; but marriage involves resolving the incompatible needs of two different people.

Cecil Osborne
The Art of Understanding Your Mate

So you negotiate, you clarify, and settle in. You find your position, you fix your pillows, and arrange your mutual blanket.

That blanket, essentially *is* your relationship: one big cover concealing the fact that two people are inside, squirming around each other trying to get comfortable.

Paul Reiser
Couplehood

CHURCHES are not destroyed by differences. Families are not destroyed by differences. Marriages are not destroyed by differences. They are destroyed by the immature, irresponsible, and unhealthy ways we choose to respond to those differences.

H. Norman Wright and Gary J. Oliver
How to Change Your Spouse (Without Ruining Your Marriage)

Through **Dangers** and **Threats**

THE Lord Almighty [says,] "So guard yourself;
always remain loyal to your wife."

Malachi 2:16b

A SIMPLE enough pleasure, surely, to have
breakfast alone with one's husband, but how
seldom married people in the midst of life
achieve it.

Anne Morrow Lindbergh
Gift from the Sea

WHEN two caring people who are committed to each other wrestle with the inevitable hard times that confront every married couple, in a spirit of kindness and tenderness and forgiveness, miracles do happen.

Dale Evans Rogers
God in the Hard Times

THE place to start saving marriages is with your own marriage. You might not be able to save the marriage of your next-door neighbor, but you can concentrate on not only saving, but improving, your own. If everyone would work objectively and consistently on his or her own marriage, just think what it would do to the statistics—and to the homes.

Janette Oke
in *Three Essentials for a Successful Marriage*

WHEN you said "I do," you probably took for granted that "we will." But it's up to you to emphasize the long-term view, to guard your heart and mind when attracted to alternatives, and to work at approaching life as a team. The commitment of constraint may keep you married, but it won't keep you together the way you deeply desire. That's a job for dedication.

Scott Stanley
"Commitment Isn't Everything," *Marriage Partnership* magazine

SO many people think divorce a panacea for every ill, find out, when they try it, that the remedy is worse than the disease.

Dorothy Dix
Dorothy Dix, Her Book

LIKING your mate as a person greatly facilitates working through the problems of both marriage and life.

Jeanette and Robert Lauer
'Til Death Do Us Part

THE great secret of successful marriage is to treat all disasters as incidents, and none of the incidents as disasters.

Harold Nicolson
in *20,000 Quips and Quotes* (Evan Esar, ed.)

SELFISHNESS probably kills more marriages than anything else, including adultery (which is selfishness crawling along slimy depths). Selfishness speaks of *my* identity, *my* rights, *my* fulfillment, *my* happiness.

Elizabeth Cody Newenhuyse
"Serving Time on the California Coast," *Marriage Partnership* magazine

THERE is such a thing as creeping separateness. What do young people who are freshly married do? They can't rest when they're apart. They want to be together all the time. But they develop separate interests, especially if they have separate jobs and some separate friends. So they drift apart. Pretty soon they have little in common except, maybe, the children. So the stage is set for one of them to fall in love with someone else. Later they'll say that the reason for the divorce was that he/she fell in love with someone else, but it wasn't that at all. It was because they let themselves grow apart.

Sheldon Vanauken
The Door Interviews

WE saw so many marriages around us in trouble; the problem was they didn't know how to communicate. We didn't want to fool ourselves and think it couldn't happen to us. We struggle and mess up and are fragile like anybody else. We started going to a counselor before there was a big blowup. I'm real thankful we did that.

Michael Card
Virtue magazine (Nov/Dec 1997)

OUR second year together, when the word *divorce* slipped into arguments as the ultimate trump card, we agreed to disarm that power. We promised never to wield the word as a threat or a weapon. I am glad. At times, we have both considered the prospect of life apart. We have gone to marriage counseling. We have paid our dues. But today, this day, I do not wish to dwell on those stormy times. What strikes me above all—and I say this with humility and gratitude to God—is that out of all the struggle, great good has come.

Philip Yancey
"My Legs Ache, but We Made It," *Christianity Today* magazine

I SOMETIMES wonder if the Christian work ethic hasn't been the indirect cause of our marital stress. Surely God, who created marriage, didn't give Adam and Eve such a long list of chores to accomplish in the garden that they had no time to enjoy each other and their surroundings. He's given us nice surroundings, a roomy house, two great kids. . . . I wonder if we seem ungrateful when we become so wrapped up in caring for and maintaining our house that we fail to work on our home?

Vicki Huffman
"A Marriage Sabbath," *Virtue* magazine

Taking On the Tough Times

THE amount of conflict in a marriage only
determines the speed at which the marriage is
moving toward greatness or toward destruction.

Neil Clark Warren
"Work It Out," *Focus on the Family* magazine

$\mathcal{T}$HERE are a lot of marriages today that break up just at the point where they could mature and deepen. We are taught to quit when it hurts. But often, it is the times of pain that produce the most growth in a relationship.

Madeleine L'Engle
The Door Interviews

$\mathcal{T}$HERE is no such thing as a home completely without conflicts. The last couple to live "happily ever after" was Snow White and Prince Charming. Even though you are committed to your mate, there will still be times of tension, tears, struggle, disagreement, and impatience. Commitment doesn't erase our humanity! That's bad news, but it's realistic.

Charles Swindoll
Commitment: The Key to Marriage

$\mathcal{W}$HILE the marriage vow cannot guarantee that we will always handle everything that comes up, it does signal our intention to make the attempt.

John Welwood
Journey of the Heart: Intimate Relationships and the Path of Love

Bruce lost his job. Bills went unpaid. The kids' orthodontist was dismissed. There was no new dress for my mom's funeral. When I was feeling really low one day, Bruce brought home one yellow rose, my favorite. In a few days, after returning from a discouraging job interview, he left another rose in a vase on the kitchen table. When one wilted, another appeared in its place. I objected and told Bruce that our budget simply would not allow frivolities.

"Flowers always make a good day," he said. I knew he was right. My wonderful guy explained that just because everything in our lives wasn't perfect didn't mean we couldn't enjoy ourselves. Bruce still doesn't have a job, but usually we have a fresh yellow rose on the table anyway. Sometimes I am the one who digs around in the bottom of my purse or wallet or down into the depths of the recliner looking for fallen change. When I find it, I fly off to the local discount florist. I think it lets Bruce know that I believe in him, no matter what.

This one little effort has raised the morale of our whole family during this difficult time of unemployment and has had a calming effect. Even the kids have become Dad's cheerleaders by picking a daisy or dandelion to stick in the "high hopes" vase now and then. The sunny spot on the kitchen table helps us remember we are all in this struggle together and reminds us how glad we are for each other. Those flowers will remain a part of our lives no matter how tight things get.

Woman
in *400 More Creative Ways to Say I Love You*

𝕸OST couples contend with some trait or circumstance that won't seem to go away, no matter what they do. Courage calls us to accept the malady, as Paul did his mysterious affliction, and lean hard on God's grace for the strength to endure what we neither deserve nor entirely welcome.

Diane Eble
"Marriage Ain't for Wimps," *Marriage Partnership* magazine

𝖂HEN we were married we made promises, and we took them seriously. . . . There've been a number of times in my marriage when—if I hadn't made promises—I'd have quit. . . . I'm not an easy person to live with.

Madeleine L'Engle
A Circle of Quiet

WE have removed the term "divorce" from our vocabulary when we are working through a tough time. We do not refer to it, we do not use it as a threat, nor do we tuck it away in a safe place in our minds for some future use.

Charles Swindoll
Strike the Original Match

BLESSED are the man and the woman who have grown beyond themselves and have seen through their separations. They delight in the way things are and keep their hearts open, day and night. They are like trees planted near flowing rivers, which bear fruit when they are ready. Their leaves will not fall or wither. Everything they do will succeed.

Psalm 1:1-3
adapted by Stephen Mitchell, in *Into the Garden: A Wedding Anthology*

ALL couples struggle; all couples need God's transforming power. And every couple—even those whose marriages have been difficult from the start—share the biggest, most glaring road sign of the marriage experience: their wedding vows. God goes to great lengths to honor the vows made between men and women.

Paul Kortepeter
"Ridin' on the Freeway of Love," *Marriage Partnership* magazine

𝒜 MARRIAGE without a sense of humor is like a wagon without springs—jolted by every bump in the road.

Henry Ward Beecher
Becoming Soul Mates

Repentance & Forgiveness

A HAPPY marriage is the union of two good forgivers.

Robert Quillen
in Family Traditions That Last a Lifetime

INSTEAD, be kind to each other, tenderhearted, forgiving one another, just as God through Christ has forgiven you.

Ephesians 4:32

AT a dinner party one night Lady Churchill was seated across the table from Sir Winston, who kept making his hand walk up and down—two fingers bent at the knuckles. The fingers appeared to be walking toward Lady Churchill. Finally, her dinner partner asked, "Why is Sir Winston looking at you so wistfully, and whatever is he doing with those two knuckles on the table?"

"That's simple," she replied. "We had a mild quarrel before we left home, and he is indicating it's his fault and he's on his knees to me in abject apology."

Allen T. Edmunds
in *Reader's Digest* (January 1982)

DON'T let the sun go down while you are still angry.

Ephesians 4:26b

"I can forgive, but I cannot forget" is only another way of saying, "I will not forgive." Forgiveness ought to be like a cancelled note— torn in two and burned up, so that it never can be shown against one.

Henry Ward Beecher

WHEN it comes to marriage, scorekeeping isn't funny. Not only does it draw the lines of battle, but it can destroy emotional intimacy faster than a badly timed phone call destroys intimacy.

Eileen Silva Kindig
"The 50-50 Trap," *Marriage Partnership* magazine

A FEW things never will be different simply because the other one doesn't see the value of change. Jim gets his own Sunday night supper but always forgets to wipe up the kitchen counter, although I have asked and asked. I finally concluded that quietly doing that little task myself wouldn't take more than forty-five minutes out of my entire life. Later, in a month, when I forgot to fill the car gas tank for the fifth time and Jim pretended not to notice, I was reminded of the wisdom of a forgiving attitude. We both mean well.

Marnie
in *400 More Creative Ways to Say I Love You*

LORD, when we are wrong, make us willing to change, and when we are right, make us easy to live with.

Peter Marshall

$\mathcal{Y}$OU can bear your own faults, and why not a fault in your wife?

Benjamin Franklin
Poor Richard's Almanac

$\mathcal{T}$HE focus shouldn't be on a quid-pro-quo relationship, but on the marriage vows. When we keep score, we automatically see the other person as the problem and absolve ourselves from guilt.

Eileen Silva Kindig
"The 50-50 Trap," *Marriage Partnership* magazine

A Picture of Marriage

IN fact, there are three complete beings in a marriage—you, your spouse, and the relationship between you, which both of you serve, which benefits each of you, but which is not exactly like either one of you.

Walter Wangerin Jr.
As for Me and My House

SOMETIMES idiosyncrasies which used to be irritating become endearing, part of the complexity of a partner who has become woven deep into our own selves.

Madeleine L'Engle
Two-Part Invention

IF kissing and being engaged were this inflammatory, marriage must burn clear to the bone. I wondered how flesh and blood could endure the ecstasy. How did married couples manage to look so calm and unexcited?

Jessamyn West
The Life I Really Lived

BISHOP: Who is it that sees and hears all we do, and before whom even I am but as a crushed worm?
Page: The Missus, my lord.

Punch (Vol. 19, 1880)

ART Sueltz has satirized a common marriage problem by chronicling the stages of the common cold in seven years of marriage:

First year: "Sugar, I'm worried about my little baby girl. You've got a bad sniffle. I want to put you in a hospital for a complete checkup. I know the food is lousy, so I've arranged for your meals to be sent up from Rossini's."

Second year: "Listen, honey, I don't like the sound of that cough. I've called Dr. Miller and he's going to rush right over. Now will you go to bed like a good girl just for me, please?"

Third year: "Maybe you'd better lie down, honey. Nothing like a little rest if you're feeling bad. I'll bring you something to eat. Have we got any soup in the house?"

Fourth year: "Look, dear. Be sensible. After you've fed the kids and washed the dishes, you'd better hit the sack."

Fifth year: "Why don't you take a couple aspirin?"

Sixth year: "If you'd just gargle or something instead of sitting around barking like a seal."

Seventh year: "For heaven's sake, stop sneezing. What are you trying to do, give me pneumonia?"

Arthur Sueltz
Life at Close Quarters

$\mathcal{B}$EFORE marriage, a man will lie awake all night thinking about something you said; after marriage, he'll fall asleep before you finish saying it.

Helen Rowland

in God's Little Devotional Book for Dads

$\mathcal{I}$ LOVE seeing couples who have been together for fifty years or more. Their lives speak of commitment that makes me know it is possible to love someone through thick and thin, for a long, long time.

I know of a couple who have stayed married for sixty years. They were married just after the Great Depression. She was sixteen and he was twenty-six. He was told that she was much too young, that he was robbing the cradle. She probably was too young. She had her first child when she was eighteen. I marvel that they made it.

They have been through a lot of life together . . . postdepression days, World War II, fires, accidents, surgeries, near bankruptcy, and family deaths. They have logged many miles, sometimes moving from state to state looking for work, and even living once in a tent.

They speak now of the many good times together. They have no remorse about the relationship or the life they have lived. They take pride in their children and grandchildren. I notice they most often look at each other in very caring ways and frequently speak in tones of understanding and gentleness.

I know these people well. They are my parents, Harold and Betty, and I have been able to observe this union from the inside. Harold and Betty's love is committed love.

Bill Carmichael

Lifetime Partner

IT is immature to think that the person I married thirty years ago, when she was eighteen, is the same person now at the age of forty-eight. It is unfair for me to hold her to some youthful expectation I may have had about our relationship. We both have made significant changes— physically, emotionally, spiritually, vocationally. We are different people. Life has developed us, shaped us, molded us . . . hopefully for the better.

Bill Carmichael

$\mathcal{A}$ WIFE is married to her husband as long as he lives.

1 Corinthians 7:39a

$\mathcal{T}$HERE is nothing more lovely in life than the union of two people whose love for one another has grown through the years from the small acorn of passion into a great rooted tree. Surviving all vicissitudes, and rich with its manifold branches, every leaf holding its own significance.

Vita Sackville-West
No Signposts in the Sea

$\mathcal{F}$OR forty years my act consisted of one joke. And then she died. Gracie was my partner in our act, my best friend, my wife and my lover, and the mother of our two children. We were a team, both on and off the stage. Our relationship was simple: I fed her the straight lines and she fed me. She made me famous as the only man in America who could get a laugh by complaining, "My wife understands me."

We had a good marriage. We knew it was a good marriage because we never read anything bad about it in the papers. They only wrote about

us once in the big gossip magazine, *Confidential*.
They wrote a story that said we'd had a big fight
and I'd moved into the west wing of our house.
I knew that couldn't be true—our house didn't
have a west wing.

George Burns
Gracie: A Love Story

NO one knows us better than our spouse—and
no one knows better the things we are in denial
about.

David Stoop
Seeking God Together

WE feasted on love—every mode of it—solemn
and merry, romantic and realistic, sometimes
as dramatic as a thunderstorm, sometimes as
comfortable and unemphatic as putting on your
soft slippers.

C. S. Lewis
in *C. S. Lewis through the Shadowlands*

WHATEVER you may look like, marry a man
your own age—as your beauty fades—so will his
eyesight.

Phyllis Diller

*M*ARRIAGE can survive even the decline of physical passion if interests that are far more valuable take its place.

Honore de Balzac
The Memoirs of Two Young Wives

*N*O one talks about fidelity anymore; it's just something you hope is still around . . . and in significant numbers. And when the Coast Guard band strikes up "Semper Fidelis" and your husband says, "They're playing our song. You wanta dance?" you know you're married.

Erma Bombeck
If Life Is a Bowl of Cherries—What Am I Doing in the Pits?

*N*O man knows who the wife of his bosom is until he has gone with her through the fiery trials of this world.

Washington Irving

*D*EATH has sealed off those married years like a capped bottle of perfume. Our marriage cannot be lost or shattered. Nothing can touch it now. It's safe—one of my treasures laid up in heaven where no mothy resentment or rusty dissolution can erode it. In a sense our marriage was like a flower that matured into a fruit, sweet and wholesome, and I am like a seed dropped from that mature fruit, now withered and dead. I am the result of a long relationship and I want to fall in good ground and produce more fruit—of what kind God and I will have to determine.

Luci Shaw
God in the Dark

I ONCE knew a very old married couple who radiated a tremendous happiness. The wife especially, who was almost unable to move because of old age and illness and in whose kind old face the joys and sufferings of many years etched a hundred lines, was filled with such a gratitude for life that I was touched to the quick. Involuntarily, I asked myself what could possibly be the source of this kindly person's radiance. In every other respect they were common people, and their room indicated only the most modest comfort. But suddenly I knew where it all came from, for I saw those two speaking to each other, and their eyes hanging upon each other. All at once it became clear to me that this woman was dearly loved.

It was not because she was a cheerful and pleasant person that she was loved by her husband all those years. It was the other way around. Because she was so loved, she became the person I saw before me.

Helmut Thielicke
How the World Began

NO married couple can calculate the debt they owe each other. It is an infinite sum and can only be paid in eternity.

Johann Wolfgang von Goethe

Parenting

A Child

Arrives

BABIES are such a nice way to start people.

Unknown

IT sometimes happens, even in the best of families, that a baby is born. This is not necessarily cause for alarm. The important thing is to keep your wits about you and borrow some money.

Elinor Goulding Smith

The Complete Book of Absolutely Perfect Baby and Child Care

LIFE is a flame that is always burning itself out, but it catches fire again every time a child is born.

George Bernard Shaw
On Raising Children

A BABY is God's opinion that the world should go on.

Carl Sandburg

IN point of fact, we are all born rude. No infant ever appeared yet with the grace to understand how inconsiderate it is to disturb others in the middle of the night.

Judith Martin
Common Courtesy

WE are born helpless. As soon as we are fully conscious, we discover loneliness. We need others physically, emotionally, intellectually; we need them if we are to know anything, even ourselves.

C. S. Lewis

$\mathfrak{S}$INCE I'm telling the truth, I have to admit that [our adopted son] Ronnie was an ugly baby. People say all babies look like Winston Churchill; Ronnie made Winston Churchill look handsome. Ronnie looked like a wrinkled little man with a funny-shaped head. "Look, you know I don't mind responsibility," I said, "but, Gracie, why'd you pick him?"

"I just fell in love with his eyes," she said.

Gracie was right. I looked him right in the eyes and he had me exactly where he wanted me. Paying the bills.

George Burns
Gracie: A Love Story

$\mathfrak{W}$HEN journalist Bob Greene was first asked by others how it felt to be a new father, he recalls: "I've been spending time on the road ever since I started working for a living. I've complained about it a lot, but I've really liked the idea of it. Going into different cities, sleeping in hotels, meeting strange people . . . I've really liked it.

"Now, though, when I'm gone . . . I physically *ache* for missing my daughter. It never seems that any story is important enough to make me not see her for another day. I know I still go out on the road all the time—I wonder if I'm fooling myself—

but missing her is not some vague concept in my mind. It actually hurts when I think that she's at home and I'm not with her. Sometimes I fall asleep thinking about it."

Bob Greene
Good Morning, Merry Sunshine

AFTER a year, when the late-night nursings were beginning to exhaust my wife, Mary, I knew it was time for Dad to take over. One night, when John-Miguel's cries began, I rolled out of the sack and stumbled into John-Miguel's bedroom. . . . "Daddy's here! It's OK!" To my pleasant surprise, the room fell silent. *Well, that wasn't so hard!* I thought and confidently stepped toward the crib.

"MOMMMYYY!" Shattering my eardrums along with my ego, the cry blasted forth with renewed vigor.

Week after week, bottle after bottle, I pushed on through the cries for Mommy—dutifully, if not lovingly. Soon, however, I began to enjoy just holding my little son. Before long, I was praying for him, even singing my prayers softly at times. On a few especially tough nights, we walked out onto the patio, under the stars, and talked about moons and dogs and raisin bread.

And then late one night, it happened.

Lost in heavy sleep, I stirred as a strange sound tapped lightly on my ear.

"Daa-dee . . ."

My eyes flickered open, closed again. Shifting, I reached to pull the covers higher.

"DA-DEE! DAA-DEEEE!"

Bold and full-throated, the small voice pierced the dark morning stillness like a bugle.

My eyes exploded open. Lurching from the bed, I raced into John-Miguel's room and scooped him up in my arms. "That's my man!" I cried out, laughing and lifting him high above my head. "Hallelujah! That's my man!"

Gordon Dalbey
"The Cry for Daddy," *Focus on the Family* magazine

EVERYBODY knows how to raise children, except people who have them.

P. J. O'Rourke
The Bachelor Home Companion

BEFORE I got married, I had six theories about bringing up children; now I have six children and no theories.

Lord Rochester

The Blessing
of a Child

𝕴 LOVE preschool children. I love the way they act. I love the way their minds work. I love the freshness with which they approach life. But a toddler . . . can also be extremely frustrating. He harbors a passion to kill things, spill things, crush things, flush things, fall off things, and eat horrible things. Tell me why it is that a toddler will gag over a perfectly wonderful breakfast of ham, eggs, biscuits, juice and jelly. But then he will enthusiastically drink the dog's water and play in the toilet. Truly, he is his mother's greatest challenge . . . and her most inexpressible joy.

Dr. James Dobson
Turn Your Heart toward Home film series

WHY are the thoughts of children so delightful to us grown-ups? I think it's because of the vast gulf between their world and ours. Where we adults see the tired old commonplace of everyday life, these *babes* see a freshness, a wonderland waiting to be explored. They are wiser than we, in a way . . . because we have forgotten the magic of things, the wonder all around us.

Art Linkletter
Kids Say the Darndest Things!

I WAS the only child in our family who was born into a Christian home, so my mother used to call me her Jesus-boy. Because of a birth defect in my neck, my head was permanently tilted to one side. I was prayed for by my parents and my Uncle Don and Aunt Catherine, all very devout Christians, and God miraculously healed me. It was during this time that my parents held me up in a Bible study and dedicated my life to the Lord so that, whatever happened, my life would be used for the service of God. I guess that commitment really stuck because the presence of Jesus haunted me until I finally succumbed when I was twenty years old.

Singer Carman Licciardello
in What My Parents Did Right

ONE of the things I had to do was pray that God would give me his love for my children. Then I allowed God to open my eyes to what was beautiful in each child. Generally, the same quality that makes a child seem obnoxious has a flip side that is a wonderful quality. Randall's strong will, for instance, carried with it the ability for intense concentration.

I prayed for divine love for my children, then I watched for God to reveal to me the children's beautiful qualities.

Karen Mains
Parenting: Questions Women Ask

YOU made all the delicate, inner parts of my body and knit me together in my mother's womb. Thank you for making me so wonderfully complex! Your workmanship is marvelous—and how well I know it.

Psalm 139:13-14

SOMEWHERE . . . there is the child who will paint the greatest picture or carve the greatest statue of the age; who will deliver his country in an hour of peril; give his life for a great principle; another born more of the spirit than of the flesh who will live continually on the heights of moral being and in dying will draw others to morality. It may be that I shall preserve one of these children to the race. It is a peg big enough on which to hang a hope. For every child is a new incarnate thought of God, an ever fresh and radiant possibility.

Kate Douglas Wiggin
in *Virtue* magazine

COULD I climb to the highest place in Athens, I would lift my voice and proclaim: "Fellow citizens, why do ye turn and scrape every stone to gather wealth and take so little care of your children, to whom one day you must relinquish it all?"

Socrates

CHILDREN are a gift from the Lord.

Psalm 127:3

WE must view young people not as empty bottles to be filled, but as candles to be lit.

Robert H. Shaffer

GRANDCHILDREN are the crowning glory of the aged.

Proverbs 17:6

ONE of the luckiest things that can happen to you in life is, I think, to have a happy childhood.

Agatha Christie
An Autobiography

WHEN the children were infants we didn't want them to grow up. They were so dependent, innocent, and cute. If they had become toilet trained and swore off crying, we would have kept them just that way.

William Coleman
Engaged

GOD loved us even before he made us, but he had to make us to prove it.

Child
in Kids Say the Greatest Things about God

Life  with Children

A CHILD enters your home and makes so much noise for twenty years you can hardly stand it—then departs, leaving the house so silent you think you will go mad.

J. A. Holmes
in *Dynamic Maturity*

THE later you stay up, the earlier your child will wake up.

For a child to become clean, something else must become dirty.

Toys multiply to fill any space available.

The longer it takes to make a meal, the less your child will like it.

1001 Humorous Illustrations for Public Speaking (Michael Hodgin, ed.)

CHILDREN are natural mimics—they act like their parents in spite of every attempt to teach them good manners.

Anonymous

WHAT feeling is so nice as a child's hand in yours? So small, so soft and warm, like a kitten huddling in the shelter of your clasp.

Marjorie Holmes
Calendar of Love and Inspiration

𝔉RIENDS of a young mother with three young children were surprised when they received the following thank-you note: "Many thanks for the play pen. It is being used every day from 2 to 3 P.M. I get in it to read, and the children can't get near me."

1001 Humorous Illustrations for Public Speaking (Michael Hodgin, ed.)

𝔚HEN my mom gets sad, I tell her to think happy thoughts—like her next birthday's coming up.

Child
in *Kids Say the Greatest Things about God*

𝔄 FIVE-YEAR-OLD boy had a very precocious interest in motorcycles. Whenever he saw one, he would let out a howl of joy, accompanied by animated remarks like "Look at that! Look at that! I'm going to get a motorcycle someday." His father's answer was always the same. "Not so long as I'm alive, you won't."

One day, while the boy was talking to his friend, a brand-new, stylish bike zoomed by. He excitedly pointed it out to the boy and exclaimed, "Look at that! Look at that! I'm getting one of those—as soon as my dad dies!"

Adapted from a story by Elizabeth Leyda

$\mathfrak{A}$ SECOND honeymoon is a terrific idea—a chance for the two of you to spend some time alone, away from the numbing grind of your daily domestic routine, with nothing to distract you from days of pleasure and nights of passion except possibly the phone call from your mother asking if there is a particular pediatric surgeon you generally go to, or should she just pick one on her own.

Dave Barry
Dave Barry Turns 40

$\mathfrak{T}$HE children despise their parents until the age of forty, when they suddenly become just like them, thus preserving the system.

Quentin Crewe
in *Peter's Quotations* (Laurence J. Peter, ed.)

$\mathfrak{T}$HE best way to keep children home is to make the home atmosphere pleasant—and to let the air out of the tires.

Dorothy Parker
in *The New Yorker* magazine

"**J**F only God would lean out of heaven and tell me they are going to make it, I could relax," I complained. But God doesn't do that. He tells us to be the parents he has called us to be in his strength and promises to do his part. . . . I began to make lists all over again. One had David's name at the top, one Judy's, and one Pete's. I wrote down in my imagination all I hoped and dreamed for my children. . . . "Give me the list, Jill," I heard his voice say. . . . He helped me to release my grasp and stop clutching onto my hopes and dreams and let those same nail-pierced hands have them all.

Jill Briscoe
Marriage Matters

MANY times we consciously avoided what others had failed to avoid (for readily understandable reasons) and that was the temptation to say to our kids, "Now what do you think the people will think if they hear that you have (fill in the blank), or if they see you with (fill in the blank)?" When parents are trying desperately to corral their teens, they tend to use whatever lasso is available, only to discover that sometimes they have roped themselves. So we told the kids that they were not answerable to the church, neither were they accountable to the community; they were accountable to us as their parents, and we would commit ourselves to giving them as normal an experience as possible in the abnormal fishtank of the preacher's family.

Stuart Briscoe
Marriage Matters

$\mathfrak{I}$N spite of all the scientific knowledge to date, I have to say that the human animal cannot be the most intelligent one on earth because he is the only one who allows his offspring to come back home. Look at anything that gives birth: Eventually it will run and hide. After awhile, even a mother elephant will run away from its child and hide. And when you consider how hard it is for a mother elephant to hide, you can appreciate the depth of her motivation.

Bill Cosby
Fatherhood

$\mathfrak{T}$O some this world may seem like no place to bring up a child. And in some respects they are right. But we take that risk anyway with the comforting knowledge that it is not for this world that we prepare them.

Karen L. Tornberg
Family Traditions That Last a Lifetime

What Is a

Parent?

IT'S too bad that the most important job we have in
life—parenting—is the one we have no training for.

Nancy Reagan
My Turn

PARENTHOOD is a partnership with God. You
are not molding iron nor chiseling marble; you are
working with the Creator of the universe in shaping
human character and determining destiny.

Ruth Vaughn

PARENTS are teachers. Our children will learn from us—good or bad, positive or negative. We are their teachers whether or not we accept this responsibility.

Jean Fleming
A Mother's Heart

I HAVE learned that I am a caretaker, not a custodian.

John Gillies
in *The Making of a Marriage*

NEVER allow your child to call you by your first name. He hasn't known you long enough.

Fran Lebowitz
Social Studies

PARENTHOOD: That state of being better chaperoned than you were before marriage.

Marcelene Cox
in *Ladies' Home Journal* magazine

IT was midnight after registration day at the college when the policeman noticed a couple in a lingering embrace in the campus parking lot. Mildly surprised at the scene before the school year had even begun, he approached the car. "Sorry, officer," the driver explained. "We just left our youngest son, our baby, there in the dorm. It's the first time Mother and I have been alone for twenty-seven years."

in *Stripped Gears*, a Rotary publication

OVER the years I have learned that parenthood is much like an austere religious order, the joining of which obligates one to relinquish all claims to personal possessions.

Nancy Stahl
If It's Raining, This Must Be the Weekend

PARENTS are the bones on which children sharpen their teeth.

Peter Ustinov
Dear Me

BUT we were as gentle among you as a mother feeding and caring for her own children.

1 Thessalonians 2:7

EVERY mother is like Moses. She does not enter the Promised Land. She prepares a world she will not see.

Pope Paul VI
Conversations with Pope Paul

A MOTHER is a person who, seeing there are only four pieces of pie for five people, promptly announces she never did care for pie.

Tenneva Jordan
in *The Last Word*

GOD and mothers can fix anything . . . can't they?

Barbara Johnson
Stick a Geranium in Your Hat and Be Happy

ONE father is more than a hundred school masters.

George Herber
Outlandish Proverbs

$\mathfrak{F}$ATHERS are what give daughters away to other men who aren't nearly good enough . . . so they can have grandchildren that are smarter than anybody's.

Paul Harvey
in God's Little Devotional Book for Dads

$\mathfrak{E}$VERY dad is the family role model, whether he wants the job or not.

Dennis Rainey
Staying Close

Rewards

of Parenthood

THE greatest use of life is to spend it for something that will outlast it.

William James

IMAGINE if I hadn't had children. What a horrible thought! What on earth would I have done? How would I have managed my life? These three different beings brought into this

world by me, who have given me so much—
some pain, some angst, but so much more joy
and love. And more than that—a connection with
the future.

Lauren Bacall
Now

𝔜OUR sons weren't made to like you. That's
what grandchildren are for.

Jane Smiley
Good Will

𝔍 REMEMBER my mother's always teaching me
Bible verses. I can't think of a time in my life when
she wasn't challenging me, twisting my arm, doing
whatever it took to get me to memorize Scripture.
She would memorize with me, pretending she
didn't know the verse. Even in my adult life, when
I was traveling so much, she gave me a Bible and
wrote a little note in it to get me to memorize
Scripture. Looking back, I see how wise she was
and how much I appreciate her persistence. I just
wish she would have forced me to memorize more.

Franklin Graham
of his mother, Ruth Bell Graham, *Virtue* magazine (May/June 1995)

𝕸Y mother is the reason why I've made evangelism my focus. She pushed me to leave the bank where I was working. I responded in those early years, saying, "I'm waiting for the call." My mother, quite alarmed, replied, "The call, the call! The call was given 2,000 years ago. The Lord is waiting for the response."

Luis Palau
Virtue magazine (May/June 1995)

𝕸EN cannot be developed perfectly who have not been compelled to bring children up to manhood. You might as well say that a tree is a perfect tree without leaf or blossom, as to say that a man is a man who has gone through life without experiencing the influences that come from bending down and giving one's self up to those who are helpless and little.

Henry Ward Beecher

𝕿HERE are moments in our children's lives when they open up a shade and say, "Here I am, look in." Often these come when children are sick, when they're going to bed, or when they're in the midst of failure or exhilaration. I call those "open window moments." As difficult as it is given our busy lifestyles, we need to make a point to be available to them, because those brief, spontaneous moments are the times when they are most likely to share who they really are with us.

Gail MacDonald
Parenting: Questions Women Ask

ᗰONEY, status, career, power, and a thousand other pursuits may burn brightly for a time in our lives. But when winds of reflection clear away the smoke, nothing satisfies or fulfills a man more profoundly than the genuine love and praise of his children.

Paul Lewis
in *Family Traditions That Last a Lifetime*

CHILDREN may make a rich man poor, but they make a poor man rich.

Charles H. Spurgeon
Spurgeon's Proverbs and Sayings with Notes

The

Importance
of Parents

YOU are not only making memories . . . you are the memories. In a deep subconscious, unarticulated place a parent stays with his or her child . . . forever!

Valerie Bell
Getting Out of Your Kids' Faces and into Their Hearts

OF all the gifts that a parent can give a child, the gift of learning to make good choices is the most valuable and long-lasting.

Pat Holt and Grace Ketterman
Choices Are Not Child's Play

MY father died while I was in prison—and that was one of the toughest losses of my life. But I think he experienced the same peace I did. As I was being sentenced, his question was, "Have you told the truth?"

I told him I had. He looked at me with a confident smile. "Then you'll be all right." And he was right.

Charles Colson
in *What My Parents Did Right*

WE inherit from our ancestors gifts so often taken for granted. . . . We are links between the ages, containing past and present expectations, sacred memories and future promise. Only when we recognize that we are heirs can we truly be pioneers.

Edward C. Sellner
Mentoring

ONE generation plants the trees, the next sits in the shade.

Unknown

I READ because my father read to me. And because he'd read to me, when my time came I knew intuitively there is a torch that is supposed to be passed from one generation to the next. And through countless nights of reading, I began to realize that when enough of the torchbearers—parents and teachers—stop passing the torches, a culture begins to die.

Jim Trelease
The Read Aloud Handbook

CHILDREN learn from their parents whether life is a wonderful adventure or an endurance of one disappointment after another.

Valerie Bell
Getting Out of Your Kids' Faces and into Their Hearts

ALL that I am or hope to be I owe to my angel mother. I remember my mother's prayers and they have always followed me. They have clung to me all my life.

Abraham Lincoln

OUR kids face such criticism and so many closed doors in the mere act of being alive that we as parents need to encourage them all we can.

Gayle Roper
Who Cares?

WHERE will our country find leaders with integrity, courage, strength—all the family values—in ten, twenty, or thirty years? The answer is that you are teaching them, loving them, and raising them right now.

Barbara Bush

MOM'S belief in me goes back to before I was born. She had miscarried the child before me, and at two months into her pregnancy with me, her water broke. The doctor told her she couldn't possibly still be pregnant, but Mom told him she knew that she was! She was confined to bed for several weeks, and while she was in bed, she told God that if He would let this baby live, she would give me to the Lord.

Mark Lowry
in What My Parents Did Right

$\mathfrak{I}$ LEARNED more about Christianity from my mother than from all the theologians of England.

John Wesley

$\mathfrak{T}$HE truth is that from the day we're born until the day we die we need to feel held and contained somewhere. We can let go and become independent only when we feel sufficiently connected to other people.

Ron Taffel
Parenting by Heart

$\mathfrak{L}$IFE is no brief candle to me. It is a sort of splendid torch which I have got hold of for the moment, and I want to make it burn as brightly as possible before handing it on to future generations.

George Bernard Shaw

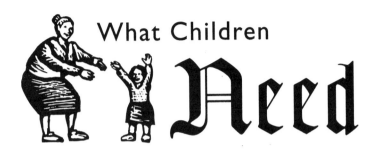

What Children Need

CHILDREN need more than food, shelter, and clothing. The bottom line is: Every child needs at least one person who's crazy about him.

Fran Stott

dean of the Erickson Institute for Advanced Study
in Child Development

$\mathfrak{I}$MAGINATION often requires some freedom of time. . . . For my daughter, there were always two time expectancies. There was my time, the now, and there was the time her imagination needed. I would say with the matter-of-fact confidence of a parent in charge of his little world, "Clean up your room."

When I went back an hour later and could see no change, I would say, in tones that indicated I was now a little less in charge, "Didn't I tell you to clean up your room?"

She would answer, in tones of a little girl in charge of things, "Well, I am cleaning it up. I have all the dolls ready for bed." Obviously, there are two different concepts of time at work here. Mine, and the one we are going to go by.

Cliff Schimmels
Oh No! Maybe My Child Is Normal!

$\mathfrak{C}$HILDREN of all ages need meaningful touch, particularly from a father. Studies show that mothers touch their children in more nurturing ways, and fathers in more playful ways. But when the children were interviewed, perhaps because it didn't happen as often, they perceived their father's touch as more nurturing.

Robert Salt
in The Gift of the Blessing

REMEMBER when we truly believed that if society treated boys and girls exactly the same, then they wouldn't be bound by sexual stereotypes, and the boys could grow up to be sensitive and the girls could grow up to be linebackers? Ha ha! Boy, were we ever idealistic! By which I mean "stupid." Because when we look at actual children, no matter how they are raised, we notice immediately that little girls are in fact smaller versions of real human beings, whereas little boys are Pod People from the Planet Destructo. I don't think society has anything to do with this. I think that if you had two desert islands, and you put girl babies on one island and boy babies on another island, and they somehow were able to survive with no help from adult society, eventually the girls would cooperate in collecting pieces of driftwood and using them to build shelters, whereas the boys would pretend that driftwood pieces were guns. (Yes, I realize they'd have no way of knowing what guns were. This would not stop them.)

Dave Barry
Dave Barry Turns 40

PARENTS have become so convinced that educators know what is best for children that they forget that they themselves are really the experts.

Marian Wright Edelman
in "Society's Pushed-Out Children," *Psychology Today* magazine

WE need to remember that adolescents are, for the most part, concrete thinkers.

I asked a class of high school sophomores what I should tell their teachers to help them teach better. I expected answers such as improved lesson planning techniques, increased use of technology, and a deeper understanding of adolescence.

Instead, the sophomore class came up with one answer, and all agreed that this was the key to good pedagogy. "Tell teachers," the students told me, "that if they write on the blackboard, they shouldn't stand in the way.". . . In short, adolescents need to see Christianity lived out. If we preach love, they need to see it. If we preach the disciplined life, they need to see it. If we preach accountability, they need to see it.

Cliff Schimmels
Moody Magazine (March 1992)

$\mathfrak{I}$ TOOK off my uniform and started for the showers, and standing over at the far wall was my dad. He had been there for 2½ hours and he had not come into my cubicle. We locked eyes. He stood up straight and said to me, "Hey, great game!" I burst into tears. Compliments from my dad never had been easy coming, and I reached out and we hugged each other. From that moment, I knew my dad.

Mark Harmon
in *Things I Should Have Said to My Father*

THE idea [of having boundaries] is not to insulate children but to equip them—not with our fragile cocoon but with the whole armor of God.

David Veerman
Parenting Passages

RULES without relationship lead to rebellion.

Josh McDowell
How to Be a Hero to Your Kids

$\mathfrak{A}$ LIMIT must be stated in a manner that is deliberately calculated to minimize resentment and to save self-esteem. The very process of limit setting should convey authority, not insult.

Haim G. Ginott
Between Parent and Child

$\mathfrak{C}$HILDREN love their parents, but they cannot handle being equal with them. Deep down they do not see themselves as grown up. . . . Teens know they need guidance and leadership. Parents, it's up to us to give it to them.

Patsy Lovell
"Hold Fast," *Focus on the Family* magazine

$\mathfrak{R}$ULES belong to life the way the scale belongs to music. And the way grammar belongs to writing. We cannot live the moral life without rules any more than we can make music without scales. Or write a story without grammar.

Lewis B. Smedes
Choices

CHILDREN very often are brought up believing they are guests in the home because they have nothing to do except live there.

G. Bowden Hunt
in *The Gift of Family*

MANUAL labor to my father was not only good and decent for its own sake, but, as he was given to saying, it straightened out one's thoughts, a contention which I have since proved on many occasions; indeed, the best antidote I know to a confused head or to tangled emotions is work with one's hands. To scrub a floor has alleviated many a broken heart and to wash and iron one's clothes brought order and clarity to many a perplexed and anxious mind.

Mary Ellen Chase
"A Goodly Fellowship," *A Man's Work Is Never Done*

WHEN Thomas Edison was working on improving his first electric light bulb, the story goes, he handed the finished bulb to a young helper, who nervously carried it upstairs, step by step. At the last possible moment, the boy dropped it—requiring the whole team to work another twenty-four hours to make a second bulb. When it was finished, Edison looked around, then handed it to the same boy. The gesture probably changed the boy's life. Edison knew that more than a bulb was at stake.

James D. Newton
The Great American Bathroom Book III

RESPECT the child. Be not too much his parent. Trespass not on his solitude.

Ralph Waldo Emerson

A CHILD needs both to be hugged and un-hugged. The hug lets her know she is valuable. The unhug lets her know that she is viable. If you're always shoving your children away, they will cling to you for love. If you're always holding them close, they will cling to you for fear.

Polly Berrien Berends
Gently Lead

A GOOD laugh is sunshine in a house.

William Thackeray

GOD is a God of laughter, as well as of prayer
. . . a God of singing, as well as of tears. God is at
home in the play of His children. He loves to hear
us laugh.

Peter Marshall

GOD is spreading grace around in the world like
a five-year-old spreads peanut butter: thickly,
sloppily, eagerly, and if we are in the back shed
trying to stay clean, we won't even get a taste.

Donna Schaper
Stripping Down

IF a parent pictures for a child that his or her
value in life is low, that child will find it difficult to
rise above these words. In one insightful study of
fathers and their daughters, it was found that these
women's achievements in life were directly related
to the level of their father's acceptance of them.

William S. Appleton
Fathers and Daughters

IN all the conversations a parent has with one's
children it seems increasingly important to me
to give children our assurance that we have
endured their same confusions and emerged to

feel the sun on our backs. I suppose, to be uncomplicated about it, I want to give my children the gift of hope.

Phyllis Theroux
Night Lights

KINDNESS is contagious. The spirit of harmony trickles down by a thousand secret channels into the inmost recesses of the household life.

Henry Van Dyke

THESE are days of warfare—a battle is being waged over your child's soul. And if you haven't smelled the smoke of battle recently, you are too far from the front lines.

Dennis Rainey
The Tribute

I BELIEVE I need to pray for my children: for their salvation, for their protection, for the development of their characters. But I also need to pray for the people who influence them daily: their teachers, their peers, their closest friends, and me.

Karen Scalf Linamen
The Parent Warrior

So, awed by the beauty and goodness of our children, dumbfounded by our failure to be the parents we hoped to be, worshiping, giving horsey rides, and picking up peas, we are brought to our knees. It is a good idea to learn to pray. As the atom is smashed to release tremendous physical energy, so through prayer we smash the limits of personal power for good and ill.

Polly Berrien Berends
Gently Lead

You know, God loves your children even more than you do. So that means He would never lead you into something that would in the long run be harmful to them.

Floyd McClung
Living on the Devil's Doorstep

In an era when many parents are protesting against laws that prohibit prayer in school, it would be revealing to survey those very parents to find out how much praying goes on at home.

Bill Carmichael

A Parent's Role

[M]Y daughter and I] were discussing the shoes
she would wear to the junior-high presentation.
I felt she simply had to wear dress shoes. She
refused with a new defiance mixed with new
fear. I felt it. After a lengthy discussion—with
intensity of feeling beyond the issue of shoes—
she wore white gym shoes. Period.

I sat in the audience as her class paraded in and climbed the risers. Valerie, shod in her flat white Keds, was the tallest and climbed nimbly to the back row. More important to my daughter than her shoes was her confusing height, her need to feel confident—all 5 feet 8 inches of her. . . . Rather than shoes, the real issues that day were "How shall I grow up, Mom?" and "Where do you fit in? You can't climb the risers for me; I have to go alone."

Miriam Neff
Christian Parenting Today magazine (Jan/Feb 1996)

𝕸Y dad is the boss . . . until Grandma comes over. Then he's just one of us.

Child
in *Kids Say the Greatest Things about God*

𝖂HEN our teenage son chose to live in rebellion against his upbringing and his faith, I remembered my mother telling me "to always try and deal with my children as God deals with me." God loves me even when I disappoint him. I tried to continue to love my son and accept him although I couldn't approve of his lifestyle. It's our responsibility to love; it's God's prerogative to change hearts.

Gigi Graham Tchividjian
Christian Parenting Today magazine (Mar/Apr 1995)

THE best time to tackle a minor problem is before he grows up.

Ray Freedman
in On Raising Children

WE expect adults to be clear on the benefits of suffering short-term for long-term payoffs. We expect adults to be role models for the children. We expect adults to teach value concepts by example and by explanation. If not, where do the children learn these lessons of conscience and courage to build character?

Laura Schlessinger
How Could You Do That?

PARENTS play a role second only to that of the Holy Spirit in building the spiritual foundation of their children's lives.

Mark Devries
Family-Based Youth Ministry

IT'S always been my feeling that God lends you your children until they're about eighteen years old. If you haven't made your points with them by then, it's too late.

Betty Ford

TELL your children about it in the years to come. Pass the awful story down from generation to generation.

Joel 1:3

THE parent [is] audience. . . . In this role we applaud our children into existence, stroke them with our eyes toward greater feats of daring that might otherwise go undone. "Watch me!" commands the five-year-old, clinging with a death grip to the edge of the swimming pool. And we do watch him as the hypotenuse between one angle of the pool and the other is negotiated. We have borne him across the deep with our eyes.

Phyllis Theroux
Night Lights

I WILL never understand children. I never pretended to. I meet mothers all the time who make resolutions to themselves. "I'm going to develop patience with my children and go out of my way to show them I am interested in them and what they do. I am going to understand my children." These women wind up making rag rugs, using blunt scissors. . . .

I have never understood how come a child can

climb up on the roof, scale the TV antenna and rescue the cat . . . yet cannot walk down the hallway without grabbing both walls with grubby hands for balance. Or how come a child can eat yellow snow, kiss the dog on the lips, chew gum he found in the ashtray, put his mouth over a muddy garden hose . . . and refuse to drink from a glass his brother has just used.

I firmly believe kids don't want your understanding. They want your trust, your compassion, your blinding love and your car keys, but you try to understand them and you're in big trouble. To me, they remain life's greatest mysteries.

Erma Bombeck
If Life Is a Bowl of Cherries, What Am I Doing in the Pits?

IF a child is to keep alive his inborn sense of wonder, he needs the companionship of at least one adult who can share it, rediscovering with him the joy, excitement, and mystery of the world we live in.

Rachel Carson
The Sense of Wonder

THERE is a general proverb circulating that says every boy marries his mother—or tries to. My mother's opinion meant a lot to me. . . . It has been more than thirty years since I brought by the date who would later become my wife. My mother took one look at Barbara and later said to me, "This is the one!"

"How do you know, Mom?"

"Look how she loves you. Son, I've loved you for twenty-three years. Look at her. She loves you, too. Son, you're creative and artistic and, believe me, you're going to take a lot of special understanding. I'd like knowing that when I leave you someday, you'll be alright in the hands of someone who feels about you exactly as I do!"

"But, Mom . . ."

"Son, every poet needs a pragmatist to keep his feet on solid ground."

Calvin Miller
in *What My Parents Did Right*

A Parent's Love

LET your eyes light up when your children are around. Laugh more. Tell them how empty and quiet it is when they're not there. Enjoy the things they bring to your life. Attend their activities, not as if they were compulsory for parents, but throw yourself into their lives.

Valerie Bell

Getting Out of Your Kids' Faces and into Their Hearts

𝔜EARS ago, a young mother was making her way across the hills of South Wales, carrying her tiny baby in her arms, when she was overtaken by a blinding blizzard. She never reached her destination and when the blizzard had subsided her body was found by searchers beneath a mound of snow.

But they discovered that before her death, she had taken off all her outer clothing and wrapped it about her baby. When they unwrapped the child, to their great surprise and joy, they found he was alive and well. She had mounded her body over his and given her life for her child, proving the depths of her mother love. Years later that child, David Lloyd George, grown to manhood, became prime minister of Great Britain, and, without a doubt, one of England's greatest statesmen.

Illustrations Unlimited (James S. Hewett, ed.)

𝕽ICK and I knew our parents cared for us. I remember one night when Dad, Rick, and I were playing basketball out in the yard. I'm not quite sure what prompted my father to say this to us, but he said, "You know, you guys can come to us with any problem that you have. Even if you told us that you had killed someone, it wouldn't change our love for you." That was a thunderbolt for me. I certainly was not thinking of ever killing anyone, but he used that extreme to tell us that no matter what we did, he and our mother would still love us and care for us. That impressed me.

David Nelson
in *Ozzie and Harriet Had a Scriptwriter*

𝕵 HATE to see my children suffer, but loving them means doing what is best for them, not what hurts the least.

Patti Covert
Family Life magazine

A Parent's
Character

LIVE so that when your children think of
fairness, caring, and integrity, they think of you.

H. Jackson Brown Jr.
Life's Little Instruction Book

I'M especially grateful that Mom and Dad taught
me how to confess my sins regularly to God and,
when appropriate, to neighbors. On just a few

occasions—and no more were needed!—they insisted that I return something I had wrongly taken or go back to a teacher and confess a lie. Undoubtedly that was easier because Mom and Dad apologized to us children and asked for forgiveness when they believed they had made a mistake in their parenting. That was not necessary very often, but the few times it was made a deep impression on me. And my parents also made it crystal clear that we could fail and still be loved and accepted.

Ron Sider
in What My Parents Did Right

IF parents want honest children, they should be honest themselves.

R. G. Ingersoll
How to Reform Mankind

IF children can't trust your promises, how will they learn to trust the promises of God?

Greg Johnson and Mike Yorkey

CHILDREN are unpredictable. You never know what inconsistency they're going to catch you in next.

Franklin P. Jones
in *Peter's Quotations* (Laurence J. Peter, ed.)

A RECENT survey on apostasy among college students revealed that children raised in consistently Christian homes are more likely to keep the faith. The more regular their church attendance and the later in life doubts about their faith came, the more persistent they remained in their beliefs. Those students who had abandoned their early religion cited hypocrisy, racism, dishonesty, and parents who only attended church on special occasions and holidays.

Patrick Morley
Two Part Harmony

MAYBE we should take a tip from the sparrow in the psalm. She built her nest in a place near God's altar. She lived where God lived. We parents who want to spend time with God can do so when we build a nest near him and then spend everyday moments in it with him.

Elisa Morgan
"Nesting Instinct," *Christian Parenting Today* magazine

THE real parents of our children are the ideas that govern us.

Polly Berrien Berends
Gently Lead

THE best way for a child to learn to fear God is to know a real Christian. The best way for a child to learn to pray is to live with a father and mother who know a life of friendship with God.

Johann Heinrich

HOW many mistakes I have made with children because I was fretting—concerned to the point of worry. And invariably it prompted me to unwise action: sharpness, unfair punishment, unwise discipline . . . even my attitude and tone of voice. But a mother who walks with God knows He only asks her to take care of the possible and to trust Him with the impossible; she does not need to fret.

Ruth Bell Graham
Prodigals and Those Who Love Them

NO man is poor who has a godly mother.

Abraham Lincoln

THE most important thing a father can do for his children is to love their mother.

Theodore Hesburg
in *Family Love*

THE people who influence us most are not those who buttonhole us and talk to us, but those who live their lives like the stars in heaven and the lilies in the field, perfectly, simply, and unaffectedly. Those are the lives that mold us.

Oswald Chambers
My Utmost for His Highest

FROM good parents comes a good son.

Aristotle

PITCHING great Orel Hershiser is often regarded as a role model for young people today. But who was his primary role model? In his book, *Out of the Blue,* Hershiser describes his role model as a man who was very competitive, yet generous and a gentleman. "In everything he does," says Hershiser, "he wants to win. . . . Sometimes he would compete only with himself. I saw that side of him even in how he cleaned the garage. He took care of every detail and put everything in its place.

"He always commended and rewarded those who did a good job. A perfectionist, he often demanded that a job be done repeatedly, but even so, he gave a pat on the back in encouragement. He didn't mind pain and he didn't mind work. And he had a grand habit of asking why? He was a stubborn optimist, with a never-give-up attitude. He was my father."

Orel Hershiser
Out of the Blue

IT'S important to let our kids know we are aware of our inadequacies. Tell them. You have nothing to lose in honestly admitting to them that you didn't do everything correctly as a parent. That admission may be the key to opening communication and beginning the process of healing your relationships with your kids.

Stephen Arterburn and Jim Burns
When Love Is Not Enough

IF there is anything we wish to change in the child, we should first examine it and see whether it is not something that could be better changed in ourselves.

Carl G. Jung

THERE are many ways to measure success; not the least of which is the way your child describes you when talking to a friend.

God's Little Devotional Book for Dads

IN a biblical way, as well as in the practical, instruction is what we say; influence is what we do; and image is what we are.

S. Truett Cathy
It's Easier to Succeed

A Parent's
Wisdom

ADRIAN Rogers, former president of the Southern
Baptist Convention, tells about the man who
made his sons work in the cornfields while their
peers spent the afternoon at the swimming hole.
Someone scolded the father saying, "Why do you
make those boys work so hard? You don't need
all that corn." The wise father replied, "Sir, I'm
not raising corn, I'm raising boys."

Marvin Hein
The Christian

WHEN NASA launched the first space shuttle, you can bet that they didn't tell the crew, "Let's just fly around for a while and see if we find anything interesting." While this sounds ridiculous, it's exactly what many parents do every day by not having a clear purpose for being.

Bill Carmichael

PANIC is losing your head and grounding your teenager for two years before you stop to consider who's going to stay home to enforce the punishment. *Panic* is punishing yourself more than the child.

Panic is overreacting to a fad that is only going to last two weeks anyway.

Panic is labeling a child or allowing someone else to label your child before there is enough evidence to justify the label.

In short, panic is responding abnormally to normal situations.

Cliff Schimmels
Oh No! Maybe My Child Is Normal!

ONCE I sat under a mulberry tree with some bigger kids and tried to smoke some cigarette butts that they had picked up along the curb, but

I became awfully dizzy and I sneaked home sick. It was a Tuesday, so my mother was there to take me in, which she did, and when she smelled what I had been up to, she said that any boy who got that sick from smoking needed an ice-cream cone to calm his stomach. She gave my older brother a nickel and shooed him off to the drugstore to buy me one.

Lewis B. Smedes
Shame and Grace

ℑ PRAYED for a boa constrictor, but I never got one. I think it's because my mom hates snakes. And she's prayed longer than I have.

Child
in *Kids Say the Greatest Things about God*

𝔄T some point of high dudgeon and stress your teen will almost certainly resort to that ancient *cri de coeur* "I didn't ask to be born!" For the sake of keeping on keeping on, resist the temptation to point out that he or she shares the condition of not having solicited existence with exactly every other single living soul on earth.

Stan and Jan Berenstain
What Your Parents Never Told You about Being a Mom or Dad

𝔚HEN adolescence hits, it's not like the past when every word you said was taken at face value. As this father found out, it can be very frustrating to argue logically with your teenager. Lecturing about the problems of staying out late and sleeping away the morning, he began to reprimand his son:

"You will never amount to anything until you turn over a new leaf. Remember, the early bird gets the worm."

"But, Dad," argued the son, "wasn't the *worm* stupid for getting up so early?"

Stunned by his son's logical question, the father stumbled for his reply. "Um . . . ah . . . um . . . well!" he finally shouted with confidence, "the worm hadn't been to bed; he was on his way home!"

Greg Smalley
"Why Teenagers Like to Argue," *Homes of Honor* magazine (Fall 1997)

𝔍T is normal for a small baby to cry at night and sleep during the day. Come to think of it, that's normal for a fifteen-year-old, too. . . .

It is normal for an early adolescent to resist any of your attempts to hug him and cry three days later because you don't ever hug him anymore.

Cliff Schimmels
Oh No! Maybe My Child Is Normal!

A Parent's
Involvement

THE kind of man who thinks that helping with the dishes is beneath him will also think that helping with the baby is beneath him, and then he certainly is not going to be a very successful father.

Eleanor Roosevelt

$\mathfrak{A}$S Christian parents, Barbara and I recognize the importance of protecting our children as special members of the kingdom of God. From the time our kids began watching TV, we tried not to rob them of their awe and wonder for the world by exposing them carelessly to the concerns and events of adults. They needed first to see and feel the goodness of God in the world around them.

Quentin J. Schultze
Moody Magazine (July/Aug 1996)

$\mathfrak{F}$UNCTIONAL parents are loving, firm but fair, consistent, affectionate, forgiving, sacrificial, encouraging, wise, humble, and strong. They also have date books or month-at-a-glance calendars with plenty of dates with their children already scheduled.

Kevin Leman
Bringing Up Kids without Tearing Them Down

$\mathfrak{I}$ REMEMBER my mother's prayers and they have always followed me. They have clung to me all my life.

Abraham Lincoln

"Do you know what I am?" a teenager once asked. "I'm a comma."

"What do you mean?" the listener replied.

"Well, whenever I talk to my dad, he stops talking and makes a 'comma.' But when I'm finished, he starts right up again as if I hadn't said a thing. I'm just a comma in the middle of his speeches."

Unknown

It is a wise father who knows his own child.

William Shakespeare
The Merchant of Venice

If you were going to wake up tomorrow as an infant, would *you* choose to be raised by a day-care center, nanny, or baby-sitter rather than by parents?

Don't do to your children what you wouldn't choose for yourself.

Laura Schlessinger
How Could You Do That?

𝕴 advise no one to place his child where the Scriptures do not reign paramount. Every institution in which men are not increasingly occupied with the Word of God must become corrupt.

David Barton
The Myth of Separation

𝕷ET everything take second place to our care for our children, our bringing them up in the discipline and instruction of the Lord. If from the beginning we teach them to love true wisdom, they will have greater wealth and glory than riches can provide. If a child learns a trade or is highly educated for a lucrative profession, all this is nothing compared to the art of detachment from riches; if you want to make your child rich, teach him this. . . . Don't worry about giving him an influential reputation for worldly wisdom, but ponder deeply how you can teach him to think lightly of this life's passing glories; thus he will become truly renowned and glorious.

St. John Chrysostom
On Marriage and Family Life

A Parent's
Instruction

OUR children are not treated with sufficient respect as human beings, and yet from the moment they are born they have this right to respect. We keep them children far too long, their world separate from the real world of life.

Pearl Buck
My Several Worlds

YOUR parenting style always boils down to how you used your authority over your children.

Kevin Leman
Bringing Up Kids without Tearing Them Down

IT is critical that the parents be parents and the children be children.

Frank and Mary Alice Minirth
The Passages of Marriage

TEACH your children to choose the right path, and when they are older, they will remain upon it.

Proverbs 22:6

THE cure of crime is not the electric chair, but the high chair.

J. Edgar Hoover

ALL children are artists, and it is an indictment of our culture that so many of them lose their creativity, their unfettered imaginations, as they grow older.

Madeleine L'Engle
Walking on Water: Reflections on Faith and Art

IT is easy to see that the moral sense has been bred out of certain sections of the population, like the wings have been bred off certain chickens to produce more white meat on them. This is a generation of wingless chickens.

Flannery O'Connor
in Killing the Spirit

I THINK with you, that nothing is of more importance for the public weal, than to form and train up youth in wisdom and virtue.

Benjamin Franklin
in a letter to Dr. Samuel Johnson, the first president of King's College (now Columbia University)

HOW we approach boundaries and child rearing will have enormous impact on the characters of our kids. On how they develop values. On how well they do in school. On the friends they pick. On whom they marry. And on how well they do in a career.

Henry Cloud and John Townsend
Boundaries

I THINK it's important to teach our children— as the Bible says—line upon line, precept upon precept, here a little, there a little. If you try to teach a child too rapidly, much will be lost. But the time for teaching and training is preteen. When they reach the teenage years, it's time to shut up and start listening.

Ruth Bell Graham
in Women's Wisdom through the Ages

DOES the average good education train our young people in spiritual self-preservation? Does it send them out equipped with the means of living a full and efficient spiritual life? Does it furnish them with a health-giving type of religion; that is, a solid hold on eternal realities, a view of the universe capable of withstanding hostile criticism, of supporting them in times of difficulty and of stress?

Evelyn Underhill
The Life of the Spirit

TRAIN is a word of deep importance for every parent to understand. Training is not telling, not teaching, not commanding, but something higher than all of these. It is not only telling a child what to do, but showing him how to do it and seeing that it is done.

Andrew Murray
How to Raise Your Children for Christ

TEACH your child to hold his tongue; he'll learn fast enough to speak.

Benjamin Franklin
Poor Richard's Almanac

GIVE the dreamers room. Go easy on the "shouldn'ts" and "can'ts," OK? Dreams are fragile things that have a hard time emerging in a cloud of negativism.

Charles Swindoll
The Quest for Character

PARENTS need to learn the difference between holding a hand and chaining a soul.

Unknown

MANY children are drowning in the meaninglessness of a culture that rewards greed and guile and tells them that life is about getting rather than giving.

Marian Wright Edelman
The Measure of Our Success

PARENTS who never read God's Word outside of an organized meeting of the church are not likely to sense the urgency of instructing children in the most important truth in the world. If we really believe that knowing God and His Son is the most vital experience in the world, how dare we leave the responsibility for instruction to someone else?

Gladys Hunt
Honey for a Child's Heart

WHILE others early learn to swear,
And curse, and lie, and steal;
Lord, I am taught Thy name to fear,
And do Thy holy will.

Isaac Watts
"Praise for Mercies Spiritual and Temporal"

THOSE who fear the Lord are secure; he will be a place of refuge for their children.

Proverbs 14:26

A Parent's Discipline

$\mathfrak{D}$ISCIPLINE is like the stick a tree farmer ties to a young seedling: It is a guide to growing straight that is held firm to the very small sprout and is loosened as the fledgling tree grows.

Janice Pressman
Inspiring Parenting

$\mathfrak{I}$F you refuse to discipline your children, it proves you don't love them; if you love your children, you will be prompt to discipline them.

Proverbs 13:24

$\mathfrak{D}$ISCIPLINE is demanded of the athlete to win a game. Discipline is required for the captain running his ship. Discipline is needed for the pianist to practice for the concert. . . . If parents believe standards are necessary, then discipline certainly is needed to attain them.

Gladys Brooks
in *The Gift of Family*

$\mathfrak{D}$ISCIPLINING your child tells him that you are concerned about his behavior and you care about how he acts; in other words, you love him. Most children will tell you that when grown-ups let you do anything you want, it's scary. And if they could articulate their feelings, they would say, "My parents don't care what I do, and that means they don't love me."

Dr. Lee Salk
Familyhood

$\mathbf{D}$ISCIPLINE is an external boundary, designed to develop internal boundaries in our children. It provides a structure of safety until the child has enough structure in his character to not need it. Good discipline always moves the child toward more internal structure and more responsibility.

Henry Cloud and John Townsend
Boundaries

$\mathbf{T}$HE wife of Josh McDowell relates: When we were first married, I picked up a book on marriage and read how the father protects the mother from the children. I scratched my head and thought, *What is he talking about?* It made no sense to me. But, years later, when one of the kids sassed me, Josh marched right up and said, "You might talk to your mother that way, but don't let me ever hear you talk to my wife that way!" The children understood, and it quit.

Mrs. Josh McDowell
in The Secret of Loving

$\mathbf{B}$ETTER a little chiding than a great deal of heartbreak.

William Shakespeare
The Merry Wives of Windsor

SINCE nothing is more delicate and crumbly than parental credibility, don't lay down any rules you are not prepared to enforce. Thus, "If you don't pick up this stuff, I'm going to throw it in the trash" is unlikely to be effective because any three-year-old worth his materialistic salt knows you're not going to throw away seventy-nine dollars worth of Legos. Whereas, "If you don't pick up this stuff, I'm going to put it up in the attic for a month!" might be persuasive.

Stan and Jan Berenstain
What Your Parents Never Told You about Being a Mom or Dad

THE goal of parental discipline should be the achievement of the child's self-discipline, not parental control of the child's behavior.

Janice Pressman
Inspiring Parenthood

How Do We Communicate?

J PRAISE loudly. I blame softly.

Catherine the Great
Empress of Russia

A MENTALLY impaired youngster seated
himself on the floor in a drugstore and began to
play with some of the bottles he had taken from

the shelves. The druggist ordered him to stop, then scolded him with an even sharper tone. Just then, the boy's sister came up, put her arms around him and whispered something in his ear. Right away, he put the bottles back in place. "You see," his sister explained, "he doesn't understand when you talk to him like that. I just love it into him."

Few of us respond to being scolded, pushed, driven, or harassed. Those six words, "I just love it into him," deserve to be mounted on the walls of every home in America.

R. J. Hastings
in *Illinois Baptist* magazine

𝕴T is better to bind your children to you by a feeling of respect, and by gentleness, than by fear.

Terence

𝕾HOUTING to make your kids obey is like using your horn to steer the car, and you get the same results.

1001 Humorous Illustrations for Public Speaking (Michael Hodgin, ed.)

$\mathfrak{P}$AY attention to the intensity of your criticism. No matter how concrete your message, if you rebuke a child in fury, the child is more likely to focus on your emotion than on what you say. . . . Watch your face and tone of voice when you criticize a child. Involuntary facial expressions of disdain or disgust carry powerful messages that the child is unworthy of acceptance and love.

Kathleen Cushman
"Why Shame Hurts So Much," *Parents* magazine

$\mathfrak{W}$E should not use anger so often that it becomes an expected emotion. All of us, including our kids, love emotion. Once kids get used to a particular emotion—be it shame, anger, guilt, or love—that expected emotion becomes the emotion of choice.

Foster Cline and Jim Fay
Parenting with Love and Logic

$\mathfrak{W}$HEN we deal with our children, we must remember that they are children.

Zig Ziglar
Raising Positive Kids in a Negative World

$\mathfrak{A}$ND now a word to you fathers. Don't make your children angry by the way you treat them. Rather, bring them up with the discipline and instruction approved by the Lord.

Ephesians 6:4

$\mathfrak{D}$ON'T be annoyed when your children ask impossible questions. Be proud they think you know the answers.

Illustrations Unlimited (James S. Hewett, ed.)

$\mathfrak{Y}$OU don't raise heroes, you raise sons. And if you treat them like sons, they'll turn out to be heroes, even if it's just in your own eyes.

Walter M. Schirra Sr.

$\mathfrak{C}$HILDREN'S questions must be taken seriously at the ages of two and three, or they won't be continuing to ask you at twelve and twenty-three.

Edith Schaeffer
What Is a Family?

IF we want to teach honesty, then we must be prepared to listen to bitter truths as well as to pleasant truths. If a child is to grow up honest, he must not be encouraged to lie about his feelings. It is from our reaction to his expressed feelings that the child learns whether or not honesty is the best policy. When punished for truth, children lie in self-defense.

Haim G. Ginott
Between Parent and Child

Differing

Perspectives

𝔄 LITTLE girl's essay on parents: The trouble with parents is that they are so old when we get them, it's hard to change their habits.

Barbara Johnson
I'm So Glad You Told Me What I Didn't Wanna Hear

WHEN I was a boy of fourteen, my father was so ignorant I could hardly stand to have the old man around. But when I got to be twenty-one, I was astonished at how much the old man had learned in seven years.

Mark Twain
Notebooks

I HAVE never met a child who did not feel that he is maligned, harassed and overworked and would do better if he had Mrs. Jones for a mother who loves untidiness and eats out a lot.

On the other hand, I have never met a parent who did not feel unappreciated, persecuted, servile and would have been better off with Rodney Phipps who doesn't talk with food in his mouth and bought his mother a hair dryer for Mother's Day.

In analyzing the problem of parenting and understanding children, it would seem inevitable then that this country will eventually resort to a Parental Park 'n' Swap.

Erma Bombeck
If Life Is a Bowl of Cherries, What Am I Doing in the Pits?

OH, to be only half as wonderful as my child thought I was when he was small, and only half as stupid as my teenager now thinks I am.

Rebecca Richards
in *The Last Word*

A Picture of a Child

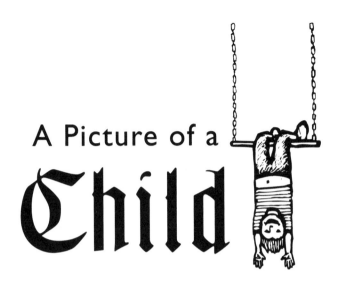

MY eight-year-old was given to me just for love because she certainly doesn't *do* anything. The new American father has more responsibilities than ever, but the children seem to have fewer. Ask any eight-year-old why she can never bring herself to do her chores and she will reply, "But I caaan't. I'm only a little person."

This little person who can jump rope nonstop

for twenty-seven minutes says that her chores are too great a strain on her fragile little body. This little person who could ride a bicycle up Mount Washington cannot muster the strength to pick up the coat and sweater she dropped on her way to the kitchen. (To be fair, she may have left that trail of clothes so she could find her way back from the kitchen.)

One day, my eight-year-old was fooling around, undoubtedly because I had told her not to fool around, and she knocked over a big bucket of popcorn. "You have to clean that up," I said. "But it's so maaany, Dad." "No, I'm afraid you have to clean it up. We're not leaving it down there for the birds."

And so, she began to pick up the popcorn. She was doing fine for five or six seconds, when she turned to me and said, "I'm so *tired,* Dad," and she started to walk away. "Come back," I said, recognizing this approach to work from my days in the Navy. "Does that look cleaned up?" "Well, I did the best I could," she replied. "It's so maaany, Dad. And my arms got tired. I think I wanna go to bed now."

I am not a physicist, but I'm sure that the theory of the conservation of energy was discovered while watching an eight-year-old pretend to work.

Bill Cosby
Fatherhood

WHEN children stop asking where they came from and start refusing to tell you where they're going, you know they're growing up.

Cornerstone magazine (December 1987)

ADOLESCENCE is perhaps nature's way of preparing parents to welcome the empty nest.

Karen Savage and Patricia Adams
The Good Stepmother

SOME children were brought to Jesus so he could lay his hands on them and pray for them. . . . Jesus said, "Let the children come to me. Don't stop them! For the Kingdom of Heaven belongs to such as these."

Matthew 19:13-14

WHEN a first-grade pupil was asked what he had learned the first day in school, he said: "First of all, I learned that my name isn't Precious—it's Henry."

Unknown

The Myth of
Quality Time

QUALITY moments with your children come out of spending as much time with them as you can.

Kevin Leman
Bringing Up Kids without Tearing Them Down

HUMAN beings, not tightly programmed by instinct like lower animals, are charged with the seemingly overwhelming responsibility of making judgments and choosing between behaviors. These decisions are made continuously—such as justifying your lack of *quantity* time with your children and family by exalting *quality* time. Quality moments require quantity time in which to occur spontaneously.

Laura Schlessinger
How Could You Do That?

𝕴 LEARNED a valuable lesson from my older daughter a few years ago. One evening I was watching my favorite television program as she was going to bed. I normally go to her bedroom and talk about the day, pray, and kiss her good night. On this night, however, she came out of her bedroom before I could get there. "If you have to wait for the commercial to kiss me good night," she said, matter-of-factly, "don't bother."

Al Menconi
Moody Magazine (March 1992)

𝕹OTORIOUSLY insensitive to subtle shifts in mood, children will persist in discussing the color of a recently sighted cement-mixer long after one's own interest in the topic has waned.

Fran Lebowitz
Metropolitan Life

$\mathfrak{M}$ANY a child watches with bewilderment as Mom and Dad ricochet from room to room in the house, speed to one meeting after another, cram down Big Macs, often dumping out religious cliches en route. Who are we kidding? Being too busy is not a friend, it's an enemy to a home. An evil, selfish, demanding force that requires things of us, things we have no business surrendering.

Charles Swindoll
Strike the Original Match

$\mathfrak{W}$HEN we're available to our children it says, "You are important." And when we're not available it says, "Oh, yes, I love you, but other things still come ahead of you. You are not really that important."

Josh McDowell
How to Be a Hero to Your Kids

$\mathfrak{J}$ REMEMBER visiting my middle son's nursery school class, at the request of his teacher, so that I could observe a "problem child" in the class. It so happened that I was sitting and observing a group of boys, including my son, who sat in a circle nearby. Their conversation went like this:

Child A: "My daddy is a doctor and he makes a lot of money and we have a swimming pool."

Child B: "My daddy is a lawyer and flies to Washington and talks to the president."

Child C: "My daddy owns a company and we have our own airplane."

Then my son (with aplomb, of course): "My daddy is here!" with a proud look in my direction.

Children regard the public presence of their parents as a visible symbol of caring and connectedness that is far more significant than any material support could ever be.

David Elkind

Redeeming
the
Time

LET every Christian father and mother
understand, when their child is three years old,
that they have done more than half of all they
will ever do for his character.

Horace Bushnell
Christian Nurture

No one who reaches the end of his life has ever looked back and said, "Oh, I wish I had spent more time at the office instead of with my kids."

Greg Johnson and Mike Yorkey
Daddy's Home

EACH second we live is a new and unique moment of the universe, a moment that will never be again. . . . And what do we teach our children? We teach them that two and two make four, and that Paris is the capital of France.

When will we also teach them what they are? We should say to each of them: Do you know what you are? You are a marvel. You are unique. In all the years that have passed, there has never been another child like you. Your legs, your arms, your clever fingers, and the way you move.

Pablo Casals

WE'RE so consumed with the feeding, the dressing, the buckling into car seats, the finding of bathrooms, and the counting of heads that we sometimes forget that there is any greater mission to raising children than making sure the crusts are cut off the sandwiches and that everybody gets a balloon.

Joyce Maynard
"Hopes and Prayers," *Parenting* magazine

CHILDREN just don't fit into a "to do" list very well. It takes time to be an effective parent when children are small. It takes time to introduce them to good books—it takes time to fly kites and play punch ball and put together jigsaw puzzles. It takes time to listen, once more, to the skinned-knee episode and talk about the bird with the broken wing. These are the building blocks of esteem, held together with the mortar of love.

As the commercial says, "Slow down, America!" What is your rush, anyway? Don't you know your children will be gone so quickly and you will have nothing but blurred memories of those years when they needed you?

Dr. James Dobson
Hide or Seek

$\mathfrak{P}$ERHAPS the most profound effect of television watching . . . is its effect on family relationships. Regular television viewing deprives families of opportunities to interact with one another.

William Kilpatrick
Why Johnny Can't Tell Right from Wrong

$\mathfrak{P}$LAYING with our children is important enough to deserve priority in our lives. It's a lot more important—and more fun—than reading every word in the newspaper or cleaning out a closet.

Linda Albert and Michael Popkin
Quality Parenting

$\mathfrak{O}$NE grandfather we know makes the rounds to his grandchildren's homes every Saturday morning to drop off doughnuts. Traditions are too significant as underpinnings to save only for major occasions.

Mimi Wilson and Mary Beth Lagerborg
Table Talk

TIMES have changed, and we can probably count on their continuing to change. So it's up to us to seek out the little pieces of life that will become our children's memories.

Sylvia Harney
Every Time I Go Home, I Break Out in Relatives

FIRST I was dying to finish high school and start college.
And then I was dying to finish college and start working.
And then I was dying to marry and have children.
And then I was dying for my children to grow old enough for school so I could return to work.
And then I was dying to retire.
And now, I am dying . . . and suddenly I realize I forgot to live.

Anonymous
in *What Every Mom Needs*

When It's All Said & Done

YOU know, once when I heard an interviewer ask George [Bush] what accomplishment he was most proud of, I wondered what would he answer? Would he say his years as a Navy pilot, a businessman, a public servant, or would he speak about some of the changes that happened since he has been president? . . . What would be his answer? Well, it's the same answer George Bush always gives—that his children still come home.

Barbara Bush

$\mathfrak{I}$F you want to grow up, grow down. Accept what you don't know. Request help. Ask questions. Resist the urge to define yourself by constant doing, doing, doing. Use commas instead of periods. Admit mistakes and apologize. Get down on the ground and get dirty.

Elisa Morgan
Christian Parenting Today magazine (Sept/Oct 1996)

$\mathcal{S}$OUND travels slowly. Sometimes the things you say when your kids are teenagers don't reach them till they're in their forties.

1001 Humorous Illustrations for Public Speaking (Michael Hodgin, ed.)

$\mathfrak{T}$HEY might not look like they have much in common—this 74-year-old and his four-year-old grandson—but they do. You'll see the similarity on a hot summer day when they peel off their T-shirts to go swimming. Each has a long dramatic scar running the length of his chest.

Danny, the four-year-old, actually got his scar after major corrective heart surgery following his first birthday. His grandfather got his last year after emergency open-heart bypass surgery.

Swapping scar stories one day, Danny asked

his grandpa, "Do you think the doctors gave us a zipper on our chests so Jesus could get into our heart easier?"

Leave it to a child to turn a traumatic event into a picture of faith. And while Danny's theological understanding reflects his age, his cute words carry a pointed challenge I'd like all of us fathers to consider. . . . How "easily opened" is your heart to the things of God? And how skillful are you becoming at opening up your child's heart to the things of God?

John Trent
Christian Parenting Today magazine (Nov/Dec 1996)

THE trouble with being a parent is that by the time we're experienced, we're unemployed.

Vern McLellan
Practical Proverbs & Wacky Wit

I USED to think how wonderful it would be to have perfect children. Now I know how much they would miss by being too good. I don't want perfect children: I want something far better for them than that! I want them to know the power of the Holy Spirit, to feel God's hand of change in their lives, and to recognize the depth of their need for the blood of Jesus Christ. I want them to know the power of renewal.

Karen Scalf Linamen
The Parent Warrior

IT would be better to be thrown into the sea with a large millstone tied around the neck than to face the punishment in store for harming one of these little ones.

Luke 17:2

CHILDREN begin by loving their parents. After a time they judge them. Rarely, if ever, do they forgive them.

Oscar Wilde
A Woman of No Importance

GIVE your children up to God. It is utterly safe to place your children in God's sure hands.

John White

IT takes courage to let our children go, but we are trustees and stewards and have to hand them back to life—to God. As the old saying puts it: "What I gave I have." We have to love them and lose them.

Alfred Torrie
Concise Dictionary of Religious Quotations

HOLD everything in your hands lightly— otherwise it hurts when God pries your fingers open.

Corrie ten Boom
in *The Gift of Family*

NO matter how old she is, a mother watches her middle-aged kids for signs of improvement.

Magnetic Graffiti Company

AND now you wear a cap and gown. As the tassel shifts, so do all of our lives, to make a way for a solo stanza in the song of your existence. Yet we always sing the choruses together—

around campfires, on beaches, in tour busses, at bedtime, in summer, at the breakfast table, after late-night dates. And the song is "joy."

Gloria Gaither, in a letter to her daughter
We Have This Moment

𝕴 HAVE tried to do what I thought you would have me do. . . . I have endeavored to use wisely and unselfishly the means that you have so unselfishly placed at my disposal. . . . In all these years of effort and striving, your own life and example have ever been to me the most powerful and stimulating influence. What you have done for humanity and business on a vast scale has impressed me profoundly. To have been a silent partner with you in carrying out these great constructive purposes and benefactions has been the supreme delight of my life.

J. D. Rockefeller Jr.
in a letter to his father

𝕴 HAVE held many things in my life and I have lost them all. But that which I have placed in God's hand, I shall possess.

Martin Luther

family

What Is a Home?

$\mathcal{I}$ READ within a poet's book
A word that starred the page,
"Stone walls do not a prison make,
Nor iron bars a cage."

Yes, that is true, and something more:
You'll find, where'er you roam,
That marble floors and gilded walls
Can never make a home.

But every house where love abides
And friendship is a guest,
Is surely home, and home, sweet home;
For there the heart can rest.

Henry Van Dyke
"Home Song"

*H*OME is eating cold watermelon together on a hot day in the backyard and building a snowman six months later in the same spot.

Home is where I discover wonder and learn to dream. It is where I find joy.

Bill and Nancie Carmichael

*T*HE family should be a closely knit group. The home should be a self-contained shelter of security; a kind of school where life's basic lessons are taught; and a kind of church where God is honored; a place where wholesome recreation and simple pleasures are enjoyed.

Billy Graham
"My Answer," syndicated newspaper column

I WONDER why it is that we are not all kinder than we are? How much the world needs it! How easily it is done! How instantaneously it acts! How infallibly it is remembered! How super-abundantly it pays itself back—for there is no debtor in the world so honorable, so superbly honorable, as love. . . . You will find as you look back upon your life that the moments that stand out, the moments when you have really lived, are the moments when you have done things in a spirit of love.

Henry Drummond
The Greatest Thing in the World

YOU know what's helped us in the Swindoll home? To think of where we live as a training place, not a showplace. The home is a laboratory where experiments are tried out. It is a place where life makes up its mind. The home is a place where a child is free to think, to talk, to try out ideas. In a scene like that, God fits very comfortably into the entire conversation. And at any place where His name is inserted, it fits.

Charles Swindoll
Growing Wise in Family Life

HOME is where families mend each other. In this place, I am welcome. I am safe.

Bill and Nancie Carmichael

HOME is the place where, when you have to go there, they have to take you in.

Robert Frost
"The Death of a Hired Man"

A Family's
Story

AFTER twenty years of wear, the worn places on the seats and scuff marks on the rungs speak of use and of life. The table, marred by model glue and a pumpkin carving knife, is haunted with memories of a host of friends and of our children from high chairs to high school. It represents the best of what we've had and of what we will have together as a family and as a team.

Mimi Wilson and Mary Beth Lagerborg
Table Talk

A LITTLE boy asked his mother where he came from, and also where she had come from as a baby. His mother gave him a tall tale about a beautiful white feathered bird. The boy ran into the next room and asked his grandmother the same question and received a variation on the bird story. He then scampered outside to his playmate with the comment, "You know, there hasn't been a normal birth in our family for three generations."

Howard Hendricks
Heaven Help the Home

A FAMILY'S history is like a novel in progress with a full cast of characters and, because each of them is a part of you, you want to know them all.

Frederick Waterman
"November Letters," *Hemisphere* magazine

NOBODY who has not been in the interior of a family can say what the difficulties of any individual of that family may be.

Jane Austen
Emma

FOR he issued his decree to Jacob; he gave his law to Israel. He commanded our ancestors to teach them to their children, so the next generation might know them— even the children not yet born— that they in turn might teach their children. So each generation can set its hope anew on God, remembering his glorious miracles and obeying his commands. Then they will not be like their ancestors— stubborn, rebellious, and unfaithful, refusing to give their hearts to God.

Psalm 78:5-8

CONSIDER history as inspiration—your family's, your country's, your religion's. I find history often beautiful and always interesting and helpful in providing perspective. It has a way of marking our place in the larger sense. It can give us a feeling like we get when we lie on our backs looking at the stars.

Elizabeth Berg
Family Traditions

THE real histories of families aren't the records of births, deaths, and marriages. They are the stories told after dessert, when the coffee's been served and everyone's too full to move.

Frederick Waterman
"November Letters," *Hemisphere* magazine

WHY pay money to have your family tree traced; go into politics and your opponents will do it for you.

Laurence J. Peter
Peter's Quotations (Laurence J. Peter, ed.)

THERE are places we all come from—deep, rooty, common places—that make us who we are. And we disdain them or treat them lightly at our peril. We turn our backs on them at the risk of self-contempt. There is a sense in which we need to go home again—and can go home again. Not to recover home, no. But to sanctify memory.

Robert Fulghum
All I Really Need to Know I Learned in Kindergarten

The Value of a Home

HOME to me is not just a roof over my head, but a dream. If I lost my home it would be like losing all my thoughts, dreams, and memories. I love everything about it, from the north of the house to the south of the house. From the east of the house to the west of the house. If a fire burned down my house, the tears would roll down my face like the water down dirty windows.

Allison Slater, age nine

in *Where the Heart Is: Reflections on the Meaning of Home*

COUNTLESS times each day a mother does what no one else can do quite so well. She wipes away a tear, whispers a word of hope, eases a child's fear. She teaches, ministers, loves, and nurtures the next generation of citizens. And she challenges and cajoles her kids to do their best and be the best. But no editorials praise these accomplishments. There are no news stories telling us that today a child was taught what it means to be loved, an infant was hugged securely, or that the wonders of the classics were introduced to a young mind. No one seems to care that a house was made a home, or that a simple table of food was transformed into a place of community and nurturing.

Dr. James Dobson
Children at Risk

BUT what on earth is half so dear—so longed for—as the hearth of home?

Emily Brontë
A Little While

WHEN I get home from a long day or hard day I like to run through my home and make sure things are the same as when I left. The power of home is beyond imagining.

Matthew Merner, age nine
in *Where the Heart Is: Reflections on the Meaning of Home*

The Ingredients of a Home

UNLESS the Lord builds a house, the work of the builders is useless.

Psalm 127:1

WHEN it comes to parenting, kids don't bloom and grow if their roots are constantly ripped out. Insecurity in a home pulls our roots; security provides the depth and shelter for them to thrive.

Gary Smalley and John Trent
The Language of Love

WHEN trying to understand God's purposes for our families, we often limit ourselves to those passages that relate specifically to husbands, wives, and children. In so doing, it is easy to overlook the fact that all of the instruction given to Christians in general can well be applied to Christians who are living together in families!

R. Ruth Barton

Becoming Women of Purpose

WE have to face the fact that either all of us are going to die together or we are going to learn to live together and if we are to live together we have to talk.

Eleanor Roosevelt

New York Times

I COULD say a thousand things to you, if I had leisure. I could dwell on the importance of piety and religion, of industry and frugality, of prudence, economy, regularity, and even government, all of which are essential to the well being of a family. But I have not time. I cannot however help repeating piety, because I think it indispensable. Religion in a family is at once its brightest ornament and its best security.

Samuel Adams
in *The Christian History of the American Revolution*

WALTER taught each of our children how to play the piano. Other instruments followed. They learned to play for the love of it. Now, as parents, they have established culture in their homes. They sit down together to nice tables, good food, conversation. These things make children feel safe.

Ingrid Trobisch
Virtue magazine (Jan/Feb 1995)

WHEN home is ruled according to God's Word, angels might be asked to stay with us, and they would not find themselves out of their element.

Charles H. Spurgeon

SHARED laughter is like family glue. It is the stuff of family well-being and all-is-well thoughts. It brings us together as few other things can.

Valerie Bell
Getting Out of Your Kids' Faces and into Their Hearts

I'M convinced there is an incredible advantage for kids who are raised in a home where they can be totally confident that Mom and Dad love each other.

Jay Kesler
"The Myth of Quality Time," *Marriage Partnership* magazine

THE greatest gift a mother and a dad can give to their children is to love each other and live together under one roof.

S. Truett Cathy
It's Easier to Succeed

The Purpose of a Home

A PARENT-teacher group was involved in a serious discussion about what the school's students could do after dismissal each day. Among the many suggestions made were playgrounds, youth huts, bicycle trails, canteens, and even a student center with a paid supervisor. Finally, a practical grandmother quietly said, "Couldn't they just go home?"

Illustrations Unlimited (James S. Hewett, ed.)

UNFORTUNATELY, many families today don't stand for anything. Neither "little churches" nor "little commonwealths," they are more like "little hotels"—places where one stays temporarily but with no particular sense of commitment.

William Kilpatrick
Why Johnny Can't Tell Right from Wrong

WHEN two people share a vision of the way things ought to be and join together in the struggle to achieve those goals, it is a powerful force. Great joy comes out of having a purpose for living. I often say that family life must be more than "us three and TV." By that I mean that the goals for living for you and your spouse and children must have a purpose beyond your own four walls . . . it must reach out to others. When we develop our purpose, we find great joy in living.

Bill Carmichael

SO commit yourselves completely to these words of mine. Teach them to your children. Talk about them when you are at home and when you are away on a journey, when you are lying down and when you are getting up again. Write them on the doorposts of your house and on your gates, so that as long as the sky remains above the earth, you and your children may flourish in the land.

Deuteronomy 11:18-21a

AS parents, Betty and I tried to give our four children both roots and wings: the roots of family, heritage and values so they'd know who they were and in what they believed; and wings, the courage to seek personal challenges and the capacity to make it on their own.

Gerald Ford
A Time to Heal

IN my home I form my view of life—what to embrace, what to abhor, what to feed my mind, and how to think. In short, home forms my character for life.

Bill and Nancie Carmichael

AND you must love the Lord your God with all your heart, all your soul, and all your strength. And you must commit yourselves wholeheartedly to these commands I am giving you today. Repeat them again and again to your children. Talk about them when you are at home and when you are away on a journey, when you are lying down and when you are getting up again. Tie them to your hands as a reminder, and wear them on your forehead. Write them on the doorposts of your house and on your gates.

Deuteronomy 6:5-9

ONCE, when our children were about five and eight, they were caught arguing. I can remember my husband stopping them and saying, "This is home. Now, outside of these four walls people are going to hurt you, they're going to call you names. But inside these four walls we build each other. Do you understand? We build each other."

And that became a by-word in our home. Are you building? Many times when Gordon or I would say something derogatory to each other, the children would say, "Mother, was that a building comment?" When everybody gets on the building bandwagon, it makes a big difference.

Gail MacDonald
Parenting: Questions Women Ask

FROM the family the child gains his first understanding of who he is and how he fits into the world around him. He can also acquire a concept of who God is, and how to relate his life to God and his purposes. The child develops values, forms dreams, molds convictions, and sets goals within the family setting. He learns how to make sound judgments and decisions, and how to view life critically. Within his family he also forms his view of what it means to be a loving, committed marriage partner and a caring, responsible parent.

Jean Fleming
A Mother's Heart

PART of a family's function is to shoulder one end of our burdens and to share the delight of our blessings.

David A. Hubbard
Is the Family Here to Stay?

THE quality of our family life, as well as our relationships with each other, our extended family, and our fellow human beings, is all directly related to our family's purpose. Home gives me a set of beliefs that are foundational to the way I view the world. These beliefs are the glass through which I look to view life, the filter by which I process all information, the formula for how I make choices and decisions.

Bill and Nancie Carmichael

CHILDREN are meant to understand compassion and comfort because they have received compassion and comfort—and this should be in the family setting. A family should be a place where comfort is experienced and understood, so that the people are prepared to give comfort to others. Comfort should be related to the word *family*.

Edith Schaeffer
What Is a Family?

YOUR children have a unique opportunity to spend close to fifteen thousand hours before the age of seven doing what they'll dream of being able to do the rest of their lives: playing. Playing is children's work. It is the way they explore the world.

Phil Phillips
52 Things for Your Kids to Do Instead of Watching TV

WHAT matters ultimately in the culture wars is what we do in our daily lives—not the big statements that we broadcast to the world at large, but the small messages we send through our families and our neighborhoods and our communities. . . . The future will depend not so much on the movers and shakers in the centers of power, but on the hopes that we generate in our own communities, our schools, our churches, synagogues, and families.

Michael Medved
in *The Devaluing of America*

I SAID to my husband one night, "I see our children as kites. You spend a lifetime trying to get them off the ground. You run with them until you're both breathless . . . they crash . . . you add a longer tail . . . they hit the rooftop . . . you pluck them out of the spouting . . . you patch and comfort, adjust and teach. You watch them lifted by the wind and assure them that someday they'll fly. . . . Finally, they're airborne, but they need more string and with each twist of the ball of twine, there is a sadness that goes with the joy because the kite becomes more distant and somehow you know it won't be long before this beautiful creature will snap the lifeline binding you together and soar as it was meant to soar—free and alone."

"That was beautiful," said my husband. "Are you finished?"

"I think so. Why?"

"Because one of your kites just crashed into the garage door with his car . . . another is landing here with three surfboards with friends on them, and the third is hung up at college and needs more string to come home for the holidays."

Erma Bombeck

If Life Is a Bowl of Cherries, What Am I Doing in the Pits?

Life with  Children

WHEN my three-year-old son was shown a portrait of his five older brothers, taken when they were much younger, he pointed and said, "Those guys are wearing my clothes!"

Victoria Ryan
in *Ladies' Home Journal* magazine

IF a growing object is both fresh and spoiled at the same time, chances are it's a child.

Anonymous

FOR the first few years after my son was born, things were fairly frictionless on the haircut front. My son favored the Dwight Eisenhower style so popular with babies, consisting of approximately eight wisps of hair occasionally festooned with creamed spinach. When he grew real hair, I'd take him to the barbershop and request that he be given a regular haircut, defined as "a haircut exactly like mine."

Then one day, when he was six, he came home from school, which is where they pick this stuff up, and announced that he wanted a punk haircut. Remembering my experiences in the sixties, I sat him down and thoughtfully explained to him that although I, personally, did not care for the punk style of haircut, the real issue here was personal freedom of choice, and since it was, after all, his hair, then by gosh if he really, really wanted to, he could get a punk haircut just as soon as I had been dead and buried for a minimum of forty-five years.

Dave Barry
Dave Barry Turns 40

CLEANING your house while the kids are still
  growing
Is like shoveling the walk before it stops
  snowing.

Phyllis Diller

Phyllis Diller's Housekeeping Hints

A LITTLE girl is out in the backyard brushing
the dog's teeth, and her father stops by and says,
"What are you doing?" She says, "Well, I'm
brushing Scruffy's teeth." She pauses and says
to her father, "Don't worry, Dad. I'll put your
toothbrush back like I always do."

Paul Harvey News (March 1988)

HAVE you ever watched a young child near a
puddle of water? Puddles attract little feet just
like a magnet attracts paper clips. It's a great
thing to watch when it isn't your kid. There it is,
a puddle just waiting there on a sidewalk for
some little kid. Then the kid appears and spots
the puddle out of the corner of his eye. He walks
up to it like he hasn't seen it. There is a moment
of slight hesitation, then the child inevitably takes
that deliberate, inquisitive step into the water.
The first tentative step is usually followed by a
second confident splash.

What happens next depends on the proximity of the parent. If there's a parent near, there comes at this point a quick and decisive reprimand. If, however, no parent is around to observe this behavior, the child can continue playing in the water to his heart's delight, without the slightest thought of the effect of puddles on shoes, socks, or any other article of clothing.

Puddles are by no means the only thing that has this effect on kids. Mud, sand, and dirt in general, often provoke very similar behavior. I have observed that many kids don't care in the least if, as a consequence of their actions, they get unbelievably dirty. Kids will even *eat* a certain amount of dirt and sand, as long as you don't serve it to them on a plate and tell them it's good for them.

Bruce Howard
You Can't Spank a Kid in a Snowsuit

ALL parents should get a list of things to tell their kids before it's too late. The following are just a few things I have come up with from experience:

Don't stick raisins up your nose.
Don't hide peas in your ears.

Don't feed the dog peanut butter.
Don't go to the bathroom in the neighbor's yard
   even if their dog goes in ours.
Don't chew gum that's already been chewed.
Don't jump in the lake with your clothes on.
Don't flush things down the toilet.
Don't cut your sister's hair.
Don't cut your own hair.
Don't beg cookies from the neighbors.
Don't use crayons on the walls.
Don't bring a dead rabbit to school for
   show-and-tell, even if it's stiff as a board.

If a complete list were to be drawn up from the cumulative experience of all parents, I'm afraid the people who read it might quit having kids altogether. Or if they did have kids, they would keep them locked in their rooms until they grew up and it was safe to let them out.

Bruce Howard
You Can't Spank a Kid in a Snowsuit

YEARS later, [when I was walking my own daughter, Judy, down the aisle], I recalled what my friend Jay Kesler had told me about giving his daughter away. He told me that when he saw that great big fellow waiting for his sweet little daughter, he thought it was like giving a

Stradivarius to a gorilla. I had shared this with Judy prior to her wedding day and reminded her of it as we started down the aisle. No wonder people were surprised to see us both laughing so heartily while stepping so majestically.

Stuart Briscoe
Marriage Matters

THERE are three ways to get something done: Do it yourself, hire someone, or forbid your kids to do it.

Monta Crane
in *God's Little Devotional Book for Dads*

A SMALL boy sat with his mother in church, listening to a sermon entitled "What Is a Christian?" The minister punctuated his talk at several key intervals by asking, "What is a Christian?" Each time, he pounded his fist on the pulpit for emphasis.

At one point, the lad whispered to his mother, "Momma, do you know? Do you know what a Christian is?"

"Yes, dear," the mother replied. "Now try to sit still and listen."

As the minister was wrapping up the sermon, once again he thundered, "What is a Christian?"

and pounded especially hard on the pulpit.

At that, the boy jumped up and cried, "Tell him, Momma, tell him!"

Don Cheadles
Wright's Secrets of Successful Humor

$\mathcal{I}$ FOUND the first few months of motherhood exhausting. Of course, well-meaning souls who observed my bloodshot eyes and down-turned mouth told me two things:

"Enjoy this time"—Give me a break. What's so enjoyable about infants who stay up all night, cry nonstop, constantly demand food, and have erratic mood swings?

"It will never be like this again"—Hogwash. When kids become teenagers, they do the very same things, only louder.

Liz Curtis Higgs
Only Angels Can Wing It

$\mathcal{R}$EMEMBER that as a teenager you are in the last stage in your life when you will be happy to hear that the phone is for you.

Fran Lebowitz
Social Studies

A MAJOR problem these days is how to save money for your children's college education when you're still paying for yours.

Anonymous

NOTHING cools ardor faster than a little voice at the door, a child who was supposed to go to sleep and for some reason has risen to haunt you. *"Little* voice?" a friend of ours laughed. "When the kids were small we laid down the law: Once you're in bed you stay there. No problem. It was when they were grown and coming home from dates or college at all hours that we got the bolt for the bedroom door. If you think a little voice wrecks the romantic mood, try 'Hi, Dad! I'm home! Don't bother to get up; I'll find something to eat in the fridge.'"

Frank & Mary Alice Minirth, Brian &
Deborah Newman, Robert & Susan Hemfelt
Passages of Marriage

Priorities

AND how do you benefit if you gain the whole world but lose your own soul in the process?

Matthew 16:26

MY parents spent a lot of time with me, and I wanted my kids to be treated with as much love and care as I got. Well, that's a noble objective . . . but to translate it into daily life, you really have to work at it.

I spent all my weekends with the kids and all my vacations. Kathi was on the swim team for seven years, and I never missed a meet. Then there were tennis matches . . . and piano recitals. I made all of them too. I was always afraid that if I missed one, Kathi might finish first or finish last and I would . . . not be there to congratulate—or console—her.

The same with Lia . . . once I picked up Lia at Brownie camp. She was six years old and came running out to the car in her new khaki uniform with an orange bandana around her neck and a little beanie on her head. She had just made it into the Potawatomi tribe. She had hoped to join the Nava-joes, as she called them, but she was turned down. Still, she was excited, and so was I. Funny thing, I missed an important meeting that day, but for the life of me I have no recollection of what it was.

Lee Iacocca

THERE are some things best done for love, not for gain. Child rearing is one of the most obvious examples. Children need to know that their parents love them unconditionally. By sacrificing a second income so one parent can be home, parents boost their children's self-esteem much more than by taking them to work once a year.

Charles Colson
Burden of Truth

NOBODY can do it all. You have to set your priorities; and if you are a mother or father, your children have to come first. My daughter was once worrying that the house needed cleaning and the beds making. I told her she could always do the vacuuming tomorrow, but your children need you today. Decide what's important and don't worry about the rest.

Barbara Bush
Virtue magazine (August 1992)

I LOVE little children, and it is not a slight thing when they, who are fresh from God, love us.

Charles Dickens

WHATEVER the activity, whether going into the hills to cut firewood, driving to the office on Saturday to pick up a computer printout, or walking to the corner convenience store for a newspaper, take one of your kids along. Make the most of every opportunity, realizing that those opportunities are finite and may never be repeated.

Gary Smalley and John Trent
Leaving the Light On

CAN you make your family a high priority and still get ahead in your career? According to a University of Pennsylvania study, making your marriage and family a high priority pays off at work.

The study tracked the earnings of workers who were first surveyed as high school seniors in 1972. The students who said they valued a strong family life ended up with higher earnings than those whose top goals included finding a steady job or having a lot of money. Researchers theorize that support from a strong family helps workers by off-setting the strain of their workplace problems.

Chicago Tribune

WHEN tackle David Williams of the Houston Oilers missed a game last year to stay at the side of his wife and newborn son, some professionals implied he was a wimp. And Houston's offensive-line coach, Bob Young, numbered among the naysayers. "This [football] is like World War II," said Young. "[If] my wife told me she was having a baby, I'd say, 'Honey, I've got to go play a football game.'"

But Williams was more than happy to go AWOL. Even when docked a week's pay, he had no regrets. The birth of his son, he said, "was the most unbelievable thing I've ever seen, and I wouldn't have missed it for anything in the world. My family comes first."

New Woman magazine

WHY should we fuss over a guest at the door but fail to acknowledge when a loved one enters? Every home needs at least one person who is custodian of the welcome!

Mimi Wilson and Mary Beth Lagerborg
Table Talk

WE flatter those we scarcely know,
We please the fleeting guest,
And deal full many a thoughtless blow
To those who love us best.

Ella Wheeler Wilcox
Life's Scars

What Is a Family?

THE Universal Declaration of Human Rights describes the family as the natural and fundamental unit of society.

United Nations

A FAMILY is a formation center for human relationships. The family is the place where the deep understanding that people are significant, important, worthwhile, with a purpose in life, should be learned at an early age.

Edith Schaeffer
What Is a Family?

HAVE you ever overheard children when they begin to brag about their families? "My daddy can beat up your daddy!"

One of the basic needs children have is to feel they belong in the family unit. Part of that need is met when they have a sense of protection in the family. An important role we have as a parent is to provide that protection.

Imagine in your mind your home is a fortified castle that is impenetrable. It provides refuge and shelter from the outside elements. Among its many rooms is a battle chamber and a jousting run for training. It also has a round table where you and your knights (family) meet regularly.

Sometimes you must lead a force to do battle against an enemy. You do so to maintain your family's respect and to defend its honor. When you return, there is celebration and much merriment. Your family feels secure and protected.

Laura Brown, Gary Chandler, Jane Swindell
A Circle of Joy

GOD places the lonely in families.

Psalm 68:6

Life in a Family

THE parents of a little boy were bound and determined to shut off their son from the influence of guns. They not only saw to it that he was not exposed to toy guns, they rigorously supervised his TV and video watching. He was allowed no cowboy pictures, no "violent" cartoons, no space operas, no anything that showed characters indulging in any activity remotely resembling gunplay.

Then, to the eternal dismay and puzzlement of his parents, one day when he was about two and a half, he started shooting people with a banana.

Stan and Jan Berenstain
What Your Parents Never Told You about Being a Mom and Dad

COMPARISON is a death knell to sibling harmony.

Elizabeth Fishel
Sisters: Love and Rivalry inside the Family and Beyond

IF you believe that your family should have at least one meal together each day and your teen is too busy before school for breakfast or at night for dinner, here is the solution: Tell your teenager that you will be glad to come to school and have lunch with him or her in the cafeteria. *He or she will be home for dinner!*

Bill Sanders
host of *Straight Talk*

PATSY Clairmont relates what she observed after her two-year-old nephew took a *purposeful* leap off the stair landing—in a walker:

I envisioned Nicholas in a pile of little broken bones. But what I met was an enraged consumer stomping up the stairs, registering the loudest complaint I ever heard. He was livid this contraption didn't fly. I tried to console him, but he was intent on revenge. He kicked the plastic a couple of times and called it names in toddler jargon. . . . I find it interesting how young we learn to blame something or someone else for our behavior, and then how long we hold onto the habit!

Patsy Clairmont
Normal Is Just a Setting on Your Dryer

EVEN when freshly washed and relieved of all obvious confections, children tend to be sticky.

Fran Lebowitz
Metropolitan Life

SOMETIMES family memories are absolutely hilarious. I think back to an incident around the Swindoll supper table:

Before supper began I suggested to Curtis (who was six) that he should serve Charissa (she was four) before he served himself. Naturally, he wondered why, since the platter of chicken sat directly in front of him . . . and he was hungry as a lion. I explained it is polite for fellas to serve girls before they served themselves. The rule sounded weird but he was willing . . . as long as she didn't take too long.

After prayer, he picked up the huge platter, held it for his sister, and asked which piece of chicken she wanted. She relished all that attention. Being quite young, however, she had no idea which piece was which. So, very seriously, she replied, "I'd like the foot."

He glanced in my direction, frowned as the hunger pains shot through his stomach, then looked back at her and said, "Uh . . . Charissa, Mother doesn't cook the foot!"

To which she replied, "Where is it?"

With increased anxiety he answered (a bit louder), "I don't know! The foot is somewhere else, not on this platter. Look, choose a piece. Hurry up."

She studied the platter and said, "OK, just give me the hand."

By now their mother and father were biting their lips to refrain from laughing out loud. We would have intervened, but decided to let them work it out alone. That's part of the training process.

"A chicken doesn't have a hand; it has a wing, Charissa."

"I hate the wing, Curtis. . . . Oh, go ahead and give me the head."

By then I was headed for the bathroom. I couldn't hold my laughter any longer. Curtis was totally beside himself. His sister was totally frustrated, not being able to get the piece she wanted.

Realizing his irritation with her and the absence of a foot or hand or head, she finally said in an exasperated tone, "Oh, all right! I'll take the belly button!"

That did it. He reached in, grabbed a piece, and said, "That's the best I can do!"

He gave her the breast, which was about as close to the belly button as he could get.

Charles Swindoll
You and Your Child

IF you don't eat at least one meal with your children, you give up your best opportunity to teach concern for the needs of others. Let's face it, chaotic meals contribute to self-orientated, pleasure-orientated values. The family meal is an excellent forum to learn about listening to others, taking turns and, in general, constraining instinctual needs in a social context.

Lawrence J. Hatterer
in Words of Wisdom

MONEY isn't everything, but it sure keeps the kids in touch!

Barbara Johnson

*Pack Up Your Gloomees in a Great Big Box,
Then Sit on the Lid and Laugh!*

YEARS ago—probably centuries ago—some woman with nothing better to do determined that food should be passed in one direction only around the table. She decided which direction that was, and families have been disagreeing about it ever since.

Sylvia Harney

Every Time I Go Home, I Break Out in Relatives

WHILE dinner should be an occasion of family harmony, all too often the evening meal is fraught with dissent. What is clearly needed is the following "Code of Behavior at Mealtime," a copy of which should be conspicuously posted in the dining room.

Cleanliness: Children are required to wash all visible moving parts, i.e., hands, faces, ears. There is nothing quite so revolting as eating opposite someone with a Chiquita banana label on his forehead.

Food: Any comments on the quantity or quality

of the food are restricted to those of an affirmative nature. Rhetorical questions such as "Why do we always have to have crummy old beets?" are detrimental to morale.

Physical Restrictions: Tipping chairs is positively disallowed, as are intricate balancing acts involving glasses of milk. Elbows and knees are to be kept off the table.

Conversation: Each member of the family may choose one topic and browbeat it for three minutes. Any topic is allowed, with the exception of those discussions beginning "Guess what I saw on the sidewalk on the way to school!"

Nancy Stahl
If It's Raining, This Must Be the Weekend

After a good dinner one can forgive anybody, even one's own relations.

Oscar Wilde
A Woman of No Importance

The  Importance
of Family

THE family is the nucleus of civilization.

Will and Ariel Durant
The Story of Civilization

I AM attached to—forever connected with—a group of people whom I did not choose. This is my family, unique with all of its warts—but mine. And without it I would not exist. I cherish it almost more than life itself.

Bill and Nancie Carmichael

WHAT we often overlook when we think of influential centers of education is that much of what we learn for life we learn as toddlers. A good bit of research in recent years has underscored this. Our basic intelligence, our capacity to understand and solve problems, together with our understanding of language and how to use it, are largely determined before we ever darken the door of a school. Long before we throw our first paper wad or spill our first inkwell, what we will become intellectually is well on the way to being decided.

It is obvious, then, that in terms of depth of impression and breadth of influence, no school, whether large, ancient, or prestigious, public or private, can compete with the home.

David A. Hubbard
Is the Family Here to Stay?

NO matter how many communes anybody invents, the family always creeps back.

Margaret Mead, anthropologist

CONCERN should be high for home and family because the world turns on the home and the church.

Howard Hendricks
Heaven Help the Home

THE family has always been the cornerstone of American society. Our families nurture, preserve, and pass on to each succeeding generation the values we share and cherish, values that are the foundation for our freedoms.

In the family we learn our first lessons of God and man, love and discipline, rights and responsibilities, human dignity, and human frailty. Our families give us daily examples of these lessons being put into practice. In raising and instructing our children, in providing personal and compassionate care for the elderly, in maintaining the spiritual strength of the religious commitment among our people—in these and other ways, America's families make immeasurable contributions to America's well-being.

Today more than ever, it is essential that these contributions not be taken for granted and that each of us remembers that the strength of our families is vital to the strength of our nation.

Former President Ronald Reagan
in *The Rebirth of America*

SOME friends of ours have eight children, and they all love ice cream. On a hot summer day, one of the younger ones declared that she wished they could eat nothing but ice cream! The others chimed agreement, and to their surprise the father said, "All right. Tomorrow you can have all the ice cream you want—nothing but ice cream!" The children squealed with delight, and could scarcely contain themselves until the next day. They came trooping down to breakfast shouting their orders for chocolate, strawberry, or vanilla ice cream—soup bowls full! Mid-morning snack—ice cream again. Lunch—ice cream, this time slightly smaller portions. When they came in for a mid-afternoon snack, their mother was just taking some fresh muffins out of the oven, and the aroma wafted through the whole house.

"Oh goody!" said little Teddy. "Fresh muffins—my favorite!" He made a move for the jam cupboard, but his mother stopped him.

"Don't you remember? It's ice cream day—nothing but ice cream."

"Oh, yeah . . ."

"Want to sit up for a bowl?"

"No thanks. Just give me a one-dip cone."

By suppertime the enthusiasm for an all-ice-cream diet had waned considerably. As they sat staring at fresh bowls of ice cream, Mary, whose suggestion had started this whole adventure, looked up at her daddy and said, "Jeepers, couldn't we just trade in this ice cream for a crust of bread?" . . .

This was a harmless adventure, which helped the children to see where their own judgment could land them, if their parents didn't do some directing.

Larry Christenson
The Christian Family

AS much as I converse with sages and heroes, they have very little of my love and admiration. I long for rural and domestic scenes, for the warbling of birds and the prattling of my children.

John Adams
in a letter to his wife (March 16, 1777)

OUR most basic instinct is not for survival, but for family. Most of us would give our own life for the survival of a family member. . . . Such a group is the basic building block of our world, the place where the miracle of "us" takes place.

Paul Pearsall
The Power of the Family

IN Berkeley, near the campus of the University of California, there's a place where the ramp goes up the freeway. Just about the time vacations begin, that ramp is loaded with college kids hitching rides. They have signs saying "Sacramento" or "L. A." and other destinations, which they hold up for the passing motorist to see and respond to. But one man was particularly impressed when he saw a young man with a sign saying simply "Mom is waiting." How could you resist?

Illustrations Unlimited (James S. Hewett, ed.)

EVEN though I was only twelve, I knew that in our family "remembering who you are" meant we were children of wonderful people with great ancestors of deep spiritual faith.

Naomi Rhode
The Gift of Family

CHILDREN need to run, jump, climb, dance, and spin till they drop. They need to go through a hunter/gatherer stage. They need to know, for example, that thousand-leggers taste awful; that ants, while they smell like grape soda, taste worse than thousand-leggers; that dust devils, while attractive and easy to catch, make you choke. Two-year-olds need to become socialized.

They need to begin constructing a model of the real world. They need to know that if you bite a sibling, the sibling will bite back; that Mommy is always good for a hug; that Daddy is almost always good for a tickle; that Gramps and Gran are always good for hugs, kisses, tickles, and lots of presents.

Stan and Jan Berenstain
What Your Parents Never Told You about Being a Mom and Dad

CHILDREN are our most valuable natural resource.

Herbert Hoover

CHILDREN are a gift from the Lord; they are a reward from him.

Psalm 127:3

RESEARCH has repeatedly shown the strong correlation between healthy family ties and positive social behavior in teenagers. They discovered that the strength of the relationship between parents and their teenagers fortifies teenagers with the courage to make wise choices. The study discovered that teenagers from close families were the least likely to be involved in high-risk behavior.

Another study showed a strong correlation between the amount of time parents spend with their teenage children and the teenager's ability to resist sexual pressure. The research indicated that all these students have one subtle and somewhat surprising factor in common: They eat dinner with their families almost every day.

Mark DeVries
Family-Based Youth Ministry

MOST gang members will tell you the reason they joined a gang was to have "family" around them.

Laura Schlessinger
How Could You Say That?

WITHOUT a family, man, alone in the world, trembles with the cold.

Andre Malraux

The Impact
of Family

A MAN and his young son were climbing a
mountain. They came to a place where the
climbing was difficult and even dangerous. The
father stopped to consider which way he should
go. He heard the boy behind him say, "Choose the
good path, Dad; I'm coming right behind you!"

Unknown

DURING his tenure as president of Princeton University, Woodrow Wilson was once asked to speak to a parents' group. He said, in part: "I get many letters from you parents about your children. You want to know why we people up here in Princeton can't make more out of them and do more for them. Let me tell you the reason we can't. It may shock you just a little, but I am not trying to be rude. The reason is that they are your sons, reared in your homes, blood of your blood, bone of your bone. They have absorbed the ideals of your homes. You have formed and fashioned them. They are your sons. In those malleable, moldable years of their lives you have forever left your imprint upon them."

God's Little Devotional Book for Dads

STUART talked about the family we might have, and we let our minds race ahead to the incredible blessing and miracle of little eternal people in the shape of boys or girls. "I'd want our kids to be part of it all," Stuart said.

"Oh yes," I echoed excitedly. "The text says, 'As for me and my house, we will serve the Lord.' I don't want to watch you doing it, without doing it myself," I told my fiancé. "And I'm sure you don't want to watch me doing my thing while you twiddle your thumbs. What's more, I'm doubly convinced we don't want our kids standing passively on the sidelines cheering us both on." We agreed we wanted the whole family caught up in the glorious possibilities of serving Christ together.

Jill Briscoe
Marriage Matters

WHEN I was little and Daddy and his desk were so big, I would go to his office and he would let me sit on top of his desk, play under it, crawl over it; I would stand on it to see out the window to watch the parades that marched down Houston's Main Street. . . . We would go on our private picnics together several times a year and it was always an occasion. Daddy and I would go to the woods and hike a bit, then build a fire and burn something for dinner and it tasted just fine to the two of us; in fact, I cannot smell meat scorched over charcoal without getting lonesome for my father.

My father loved me very much. I was lucky, I knew it. He believed in me. In return, I adored him, saw him as my hero and wanted to be like him . . . even though he was an alcoholic.

Linda Ellerbee
Move On

FOR several years, my son has taken his oldest daughter out for a "date" time, but he had never taken the two-year-old until recently. On his first "date" with the younger one, he took her out for breakfast at a local fast-food restaurant.

They had just gotten their pancakes and my son decided it would be a good time to tell this child how much he loved and appreciated her. "Jenny," he said, "I want you to know how much I love you, and how special you are to Mom and me. We prayed for you for years, and now that you're here and growing up to be such a wonderful girl, we couldn't be more proud of you."

Once he had said all this, he stopped talking and reached over for his fork to begin eating . . . but he never got the fork to his mouth. His daughter reached out her little hand and laid it on her father's hand. His eyes went to hers, and in a soft, pleading voice she said, "Longer, Daddy . . . longer." He put his fork down and proceeded to tell her some more reasons and ways they loved and appreciated her, and then he again reached for his fork. A second time . . . and a third . . . and a fourth time he heard the words, *"Longer, Daddy . . . longer."*

This father never did get much to eat that morning, but his daughter got the emotional nourishment she needed so much. In fact, a few days later, she spontaneously ran up to her mother and said, "I'm a really special daughter, Mommy. Daddy told me so."

Gary Smalley and John Trent
Leaving the Light On

ONE day your children should be able to look back and say, "My family was the one place where I felt I could be myself—and be loved for it."

Bill Hybels
Eight Traits of a Healthy Family

THE ideal place for the child is the family. When the family is such that the child cannot fit himself into it properly, he looks everywhere for some other place. The child who has been able to grow up harmoniously in a healthy home finds a welcome everywhere. In infancy all he needs is a stick placed across two chairs to make himself a house, in which he feels quite at home. Later on, wherever he goes, he will be able to make any place his own. For him, it will not be a matter of seeking, but of choosing.

Paul Tournier
A Place for You

IF mankind had not been organized into families, it would never have had the organic power to be organized into commonwealths. Human culture is handed down in the customs of countless households; it is the only way in which human culture can remain human. The households are right to confess a common loyalty or federation under some king or republic. But the king cannot be the nurse in every nursery; or even the government become the governess in every schoolroom. . . . The essential of [marriage] is that a free man and a free woman choose to found on earth the only voluntary state; the only state which creates and which loves its citizens. So long as these real responsbile beings stand together, they can survive all the vast changes, deadlocks and disappointments which make up mere political history. But if they fail each other, it is as certain as death that "the State" will fail them.

G. K. Chesterton
Brave New Family

IT is a reverent thing to see an ancient castle or building not in decay: or to see a fair timber tree sound and perfect. How much more to behold an ancient and noble family which hath stood against the waves and weathers of time.

Sir Francis Bacon
Essays

EACH family is an irreplaceable stitch in the fabric of social order. When one stitch frays, the fabric is weakened. When several stitches fray, the fabric tears. And when most of the stitches fray, the fabric disintegrates.

The sound of stitches fraying is heard every day: An anguished wife discovers her husband's adultery; a teenage girl looking for love gets pregnant; another father leaves home. These are the sounds of America's tattered families, firsthand witnesses to the rapid decline and relentless disintegration of our culture.

Dennis Rainey
One Home at a Time

How Do You Communicate?

A SEVERE test of a man's essential nature is how he appears to the members of his own family.

Maldwyn Edwards
in Gathered Gold

WE'VE long known that the child blossoms when the father loves the mother. How can the children learn to express love in a family situation? Include them when picking out Mommy's Valentine gift. Might they plan a special Mother's Day or Father's Day dinner . . . and then help buy the groceries? Encourage them to make place cards for Sunday lunch. Let them help choose the Christmas tree. Children learn love and family unity best by being part of the loving family unit.

Frank & Mary Alice Minirth, Brian & Deborah Newman, Robert and Susan Hemfelt
Passages of Marriage

A SENTENCE from Psalm 101 has been both challenging and convicting for me: "I will walk *in my house* with blameless heart" (Psalm 101:2, NIV). When God speaks to me about being more loving, this verse reminds me to make application in my family first—and then to others. It forces me to ask, "Am I more spiritual, more loving, or more fun somewhere else? Who gets my best—my family or others?"

Jean Fleming
A Mother's Heart

MAMA seemed to do only what my father wanted, and yet we lived the way my mother wanted us to live.

Lillian Hellman
An Unfinished Woman

IN the all-important world of family relations, there are other words almost as powerful as the famous "I love you." They are "Maybe you're right."

Oren Arnold
in *The Romance Factor*

Families Take Time

WHAT the very young want and urgently need, child development experts agree, is not education or socialization, but the affection and unhurried attention of their parents. The deepest problem with paid child-rearing is that someone is being asked to do for money what very few of us are able to do for any reason other than love.

"Hard Truths about Day Care," *Reader's Digest*

A LARGE majority of Americans claim that family is the most important thing in life, but surveys show that most people will put their jobs, possessions, and personal freedom before family responsibilities. If you watch what Americans do, traditional family relationships are in trouble.

American Demographics

CAMPING, hiking, and outdoor activity provide prime opportunities to bond with our families. Sitting around a campfire, walking along a mountain trail, or waiting by a lakeside for the fish to bite, offer never-to-be-duplicated moments to talk on a deeper level with our children. These special times help us understand where they are going in life and what concerns them. Just being with them communicates they are loved. A parent's willingness to wait for conversation to develop further amplifies their child's self-worth.

Gary Smalley and John Trent
Leaving the Light On

THERE is something special about camping even if it is in the backyard. Sleeping in sleeping bags in the old pup tent with a friend. Telling stories and giggling for no particular reason. I can remember as a young boy looking up at the stars and for the first time thinking about the vastness of God.

Camping with the family or with a son or daughter can be a powerful spiritual experience. There is something about listening to a hoot owl in the dark night, hearing the crackle of a midnight campfire, and smelling the scent of dew on freshened pines. It brings us closer to the Creator and farther away from worrisome distractions and pressures. It allows our sons and daughters to see, hear, and feel the majesty of God's creation.

Laura Brown, Gary Chandler, Jane Swindell
A Circle of Love

IN becoming hurried adults, we've created hurried children, robbing them of time to use their imaginations and simply be kids. Wrote *Wall Street Journal:* "If Mark Twain penned *The Adventures of Tom Sawyer* today, his barefoot hero would be shuttling between tennis camp and piano lessons instead of dreaming up pranks with his pal Huck Finn."

Bob Welsh
New Course for a Decade

$\mathbf{I}$N the West, yesterday's extended family has shrunk to today's nuclear family; social security and community affluence have reduced the family's importance as an economic unit, and all this has weakened family relationships. Parents are too busy to give time to their children, and young people, identifying with current youth culture, are more prone than ever to write off their parents as clueless old fuddy-duddies.

James Packer
Your Father Loves You

$\mathbf{W}$ITHOUT question, the most damaging isolation that teenagers in our culture experience is from their own families. American parents spend less time with their children than do parents in any other country in the world, according to Harvard psychiatrist Armand Nicholi. With one in four young people now indicating that they have *never* had a meaningful conversation with their father, is it any wonder that 76 percent of the 1,200 teens surveyed in *USA Today* actually *want* their parents to spend more time with them?

Mark DeVries
Family-Based Youth Ministry

TAKE time with your children, for the sins of a father visit in the next generation. But if your child goes astray and you have reared him according to the Word of God, the Bible says when he's old he'll come back.

Billy Graham
Answers to Life's Problems

WHEN I made the big leagues and Dad was coaching third base for the Orioles, a big deal was made about the father-son relationship. Dad always replied, "They're all my sons." People thought he was just trying to play down the situation, and he was, but he was also stating the truth. He said several times over the years that he spent more time with his players than he did with his own children, and that he feared he had neglected us at times because of his job. But I don't feel that way about Dad's absence. I missed him when he was gone, but he was always there in the way that counts. I just remember missing him sometimes.

One reason I'm so adamant today about spending as much time as possible at home with my own kids, one of the reasons I can't see myself as a manager after I retire, is that I didn't have that time with my own father. He did what he had to do to support his family, and he didn't have many options, but I do, and I'm going to make sure I'm more available for my two kids.

Cal Ripken Jr.
The Only Way I Know

Too many parents live with the regrets of abandoned moments. It takes time to be silly, to share a secret, to heal a hurt, to kiss away a tear. Moments of uninhibited communication between child and parent cannot be planned; they just happen. The only ingredient we bring to that dynamic of family life is our availability . . . and that is spelled T-I-M-E.

David Jeremiah
Exposing the Myths of Parenthood

A Picture

of a Family

$\mathbf{I}$N a home that's a refuge, chores can wait a few moments while a child strokes and confides in a cat. A father can watch television with a bowl of popcorn in his lap and choose not to answer the phone. A mother can relax in a tub undisturbed while her worries melt away.

Mimi Wilson and Mary Beth Lagerborg
Table Talk

MY children are so different you wouldn't believe they came from the same family. They didn't!

Each child is born into a uniquely different family from the others even if they have the same mother and father. When the oldest is born, there are three people in the family. The next child not only has a mother and father, but a sibling with which to have a relationship. By the time you get to number four, maybe eight years have passed. Dad is making more money, but traveling. Mom is running a car pool. Life is very different from the tranquility number one enjoyed. Add a few problems along the way like illness, the death of grandparents, a move to a new city, and you have a vastly different family.

There is nothing good or bad about this scenario. It's just different for each child. Each child will be impacted differently and will develop his own special personality.

Aren't we lucky to have so many unique relationships within one family? No two are alike. There is no room for comparison or competition. Each family member has a special place in the world and makes a special contribution to the family.

Laura Brown, Gary Chandler, Jane Swindell
A Circle of Love

BY the time the youngest children have learned to keep the house tidy, the oldest grandchildren are on hand to tear it to pieces.

Christopher Morley
Thunder on the Left

FAMILIES with babies
and families without babies
are sorry for each other.

"Words of Wisdom from Mr. Hooty," *Prior [Oklahoma] Herald*

A Family's
Character

HAPPY will that house be in which relations are formed from character.

Ralph Waldo Emerson
Society and Solitude: Domestic Life

DAD needs to show an incredible amount of respect and humor and friendship toward his mate so the kids understand their parents are sexy, they're fun, they do things together, they're best friends. Kids learn by example. If I respect Mom, they're going to respect Mom.

Tim Allen
in *TV Guide* magazine

A CHRISTIAN should so live that he would not be afraid to sell the family parrot to the town gossip.

Anonymous
in *Gathered Gold*

THE godly walk with integrity; blessed are their children after them.

Proverbs 20:7

JOHN McKay, the great football coach at the University of Southern California, was interviewed on television, and the subject of his son's athletic talent was raised. At the time, John Junior was a successful player on his dad's team. Coach McKay was asked to comment on the pride he must feel over his son's accomplishments on the field. His answer was most impressive:

"Yes, I'm pleased that John had a good season last year. He does a fine job and I *am* proud of him. But I would be just as proud if he had never played the game at all."

Dr. James Dobson
Hide or Seek

THE best place for a child to learn religious faith is at home, in the bosom of a family where faith is lived and practiced.

Dick VanDyke
Faith, Hope and Hilarity

SCRIPTURE commands us to "speak to ourselves with psalms and hymns and spiritual songs." A family that sings builds a strong spiritual bond, and creates for each individual a priceless source of comfort and godly instruction which will always be there, whether he is in touch with other Christians or in a situation where such fellowship may be impossible.

Elisabeth Elliot
in Let's Make a Memory

THE strongest spiritual fortress in America is the family. If you have taught your children to have devotions, when they get out on their own, they will stay true to the Lord. And how happy you will be to see the results that have come from your taking time with them.

   If you don't take time with your children now, then you will be forced to take time with them later. And let me tell you from my experience of working among delinquent girls, it's much better to make the time to pray with them when they are smaller.

John Benton
Do You Know Where Your Children Are?

ESTABLISH a daily family worship. Say a prayer of thanksgiving at each meal. Have a special time in the morning or evening when all the family gathers together to hear the Bible read and have prayer.

Billy Graham
"My Answer," syndicated newspaper column

A HOLY family, that make each meal a supper of the Lord.

Henry Wadsworth Longfellow
The Golden Legend

THERE is no greater opportunity to create a sense of belonging and closeness than coming before God as a family in Scripture reading, study, and prayer.

Laura Brown, Gary Chandler, Jane Swindell
A Circle of Love

THE family that prays together stays together.

Patrick Peyton
All for Her (slogan written for Catholic Family Rosary Crusade)

I HOPE it doesn't disturb you that your children pray for the bicycle, the dog, the fence, the sandpile, and all the other realities of their young lives. The problem of becoming an adult is that you get educated beyond your intelligence. A child needs to pray at the level of his own understanding and needs.

Howard Hendricks
Heaven Help the Home

Seize the Day!

I WISH I could tell this to the parents sitting out there whose own children are about to move on. I know what you're thinking, I'd say to them. The time goes so fast. They told us it would but we didn't believe them.

It's harder for me to measure time now. If you asked me now how long one day is, I'd say it depends. If a baby is two days old, one day is half its life. If a baby is one year, one day is one three-hundred-sixty-fifth of its life. So nobody can say exactly how long one day is. I tried to persuade my son Josh of the logic of my definition of time, but he has no respect for my grasp of scientific theory. I tried telling him about another scientist, the one who said when you sit next to a nice girl for two hours, you think it's only a minute, but when you sit on a hot stove for a minute, you think it's two hours. And that, said Albert Einstein, is relativity. Was my son persuaded? Yes, but not until last September, when the boy noticed that somehow summer was shorter than it used to be.

"How do you make time stay?" I asked once. Now I know better; time stays, we go.

Linda Ellerbee
Move On

SOMEDAY when the kids are grown . . . things are going to be a lot different. The garage won't be full of bikes, unfinished "experimental projects," and the rabbit cage. I'll be able to park both cars neatly in just the right places, and never again have to stumble over skateboards or rollerskates.

Someday when the kids are grown . . . the

instrument called a "telephone" will actually be available. It won't look like it's growing from a teenager's ear. It will simply hang there . . . silently and amazingly available!

Someday when the kids are grown . . . we will return to normal conversations. "Yuk!" will not be heard. "Hurry up, I gotta go!" will not accompany the banging of fists on the bathroom door. "It's my turn" won't call for a referee.

Someday when the kids are grown . . . we won't run out of toilet tissue. We won't forget to shut the refrigerator door. I won't have to answer, "Daddy, is it a sin that you're driving forty-seven in a thirty?" . . . or promise to kiss the rabbit goodnight . . . or wait up forever until they get home from dates. . . .

Yes, someday when the kids are grown, things are going to be a lot different. The phone will be strangely silent. The house will be quiet . . . and calm . . . and always clean . . . and empty . . . and filled with memories . . . and lonely . . . and we won't like it at all.

And we'll spend our time, not looking forward to "Someday" but looking back to "Yesterday."

Charles Swindoll
Come Before Winter

I'VE always been conscious that every experience and every day with my daughter is a gift. I tell my daughter I love her, every day of her life, and I frequently tell her I'm proud of her.

President Bill Clinton
in *Family Circle* magazine

WHEN I was around thirteen and my brother was ten, Father promised to take us to the circus. But at lunch, there was a phone call. Some urgent business required his attention downtown. My brother and I braced ourselves for the disappointment. Then we heard him say, "No, I won't be down. It will have to wait." When he came back to the table, Mother smiled and said, "The circus keeps coming back, you know."

"I know," said Father, "but childhood doesn't."

Arthur Gordon

SPECIAL moments won't just happen. Beautiful memories of yesterdays were once moments of todays. We have no guarantees of tomorrows, but we do have this moment.

The home is the natural habitat for growing human beings and shaping eternal souls. Whether we like it or not, we are molding lives . . . now. Let's make these precious moments count!

Gloria Gaither and Shirley Dobson
Let's Make a Memory

IT'S nine-fifteen and bedtime took too long
    (once again).
Another kiss, another glass of water, and then—
The questions come . . . the hands hold tight . . .
    the eyes are open wide.
And something in me whispers, "Now's the time . . ."

"Mommy, why did Muffy die?"
"Daddy, where's the sun?"
"Are there cats in heaven?" and
"Why did Jesus come?"

And though a whole day's dishes wait, and bills
    are piled high,
Something in me whispers, "Take the time . . ."

Take the time while they're right here by your
    side.
Take the time while their hearts are open wide.
Teach them how to love the Lord with all their
    hearts and minds.
Oh, they're only home a season . . . take the time!

From the song "Take the Time" by Paul and Teri Reisser

ANOTHER balance that is important to consider—
as your children play, fight, or squabble, and you
sigh, wish for ten years to pass, look at the clock
and wish it was night, or lie in bed wishing the day
to pass because you have the flu—is the balance
between the danger of wasting the "now," or of
considering that everything is going to be static,
with no future! It is so easy for people to let their
children grow up without being taught to think of
the preciousness of "today" and "this hour."

Edith Schaeffer
What Is a Family?

HOW about that unit called your family . . . now
there's something worth thinking about beyond
today. Where are you going? What's your game
plan for the next ten years? Given any thought to
specific objectives you want to reach—or at least
shoot for? How about selecting some priorities?

You say there's no hurry? I challenge that. These ten years will literally fly by. A decade from now you'll rip the December sheet off your calendar wondering, "How did ten years go by so fast?"

Charles Swindoll
Come Before Winter

Is this the little girl I carried?
Is this the little boy at play?
I don't remember growing older, when did they?

When did she get to be a beauty?
When did he grow to be so tall?
Wasn't it yesterday when they were small?

Sunrise, sunset; sunrise, sunset;
Swiftly fly the days.

"Sunrise, Sunset," by Sheldon Harnick

TOPICAL INDEX

NAME INDEX

SCRIPTURE INDEX

About the Authors

Bill and Nancie Carmichael, parents of five children, have been gathering marriage and family wisdom for many decades. They founded Good Family Magazines *(Virtue, Christian Parenting Today, Parents of Teenagers)* and have ministered to large audiences through speaking, writing, teaching, and counseling.

Nancie has taught Bible studies in churches and has written the Bible study column in *Virtue* for several years. *In God's Word* (Harvest House, 1989) is a compilation of those studies. She also leads an ongoing women's prison ministry as an outreach of Virtue Ministries.

Nancie has worked side by side with Bill in pastoral ministry, writing, publishing, speaking, and leading seminars. They have written several books, including

> *Answers to Questions Christian Women Are Asking* (Harvest House, 1984)
>
> *That Man: Understanding the Differences between Men and Women and How They Can Work for You* (Thomas Nelson, 1988)
>
> *Lord, Bless My Child* (Tyndale, 1995)
>
> *The Best Things Ever Said about Parenting* (Tyndale, 1996)
>
> *Habits of a Healthy Home* (Tyndale, 1997)
>
> *A House for God* (Crossway, 1998)

Bill has been a pastor, youth pastor, family counselor, teacher, editor, and writer. He is a frequent speaker in conferences and seminars, churches and ministers' institutes, as well as on radio and television talk shows, regarding family and leadership topics.